The Complete Guide to Logistics and Distribution Management

Table of Contents

Section 1: Foundations of Logistics and Distribution Management

Introduction to Logistics and Distribution Management	4
The Role of Logistics in the Supply Chain	10
Key Concepts in Distribution Management	16
Strategic Logistics Planning	23

Section 2: Core Components of Logistics and Distribution — 30

Transportation Management	31
Warehousing and Storage	39
Inventory Management	47
Order Fulfillment and Customer Service	54

Section 3: Advanced Topics in Logistics — 60

Distribution Network Design	61
Reverse Logistics	68
Cold Chain Logistics	76
Third-Party Logistics (3PL) and Fourth-Party Logistics (4PL)	84
Last-Mile Delivery	94

Section 4: Technology and Innovation in Logistics — 103

Digital Transformation in Logistics	104
Warehouse Automation and Robotics	112
Blockchain in Logistics	120
Sustainable Logistics and Green Practices	129
E-Commerce and Omnichannel Logistics	138

Section 5: Managing Operations and Risks — 147

Risk Management in Logistics — 148
Cost Management in Logistics — 157
Global Logistics and Trade Compliance — 166
Human Resources in Logistics — 176

Section 6: Future Trends and Case Studies — 185

Future Trends in Logistics and Distribution — 186
Case Studies in Logistics Excellence — 194
Developing a Logistics and Distribution Playbook — 202

Introduction to Logistics and Distribution Management

Logistics and distribution management play a pivotal role in the success of modern businesses by ensuring the seamless flow of goods, information, and services from the point of origin to the end consumer. This chapter provides an analytical and descriptive exploration of the definition and scope, the importance of logistics in modern business, and the evolution of logistics and distribution over time.

1. Definition and Scope of Logistics and Distribution Management

Logistics is often defined as the process of planning, implementing, and controlling the efficient, cost-effective flow and storage of goods, services, and information from the point of origin to the point of consumption, aligning with customer requirements. Distribution management focuses on the movement of finished goods from manufacturers to customers, emphasizing effective delivery methods and channel strategies.

Key Components of Logistics

Inbound Logistics: Managing the transportation and storage of raw materials and inputs.

Outbound Logistics: Handling the delivery of finished goods to consumers.

Reverse Logistics: Managing returns, recycling, and disposal.

Scope of Logistics and Distribution Management

The scope extends across multiple domains:

Transportation Management: Selecting optimal transport modes, routes, and scheduling.

Inventory Management: Balancing supply and demand while minimizing holding costs.

Warehousing: Ensuring proper storage, accessibility, and flow of inventory.

Information Flow: Leveraging data for decision-making, real-time tracking, and demand forecasting.

Customer Service: Meeting customer expectations in terms of delivery time, accuracy, and support.

These components collectively ensure the seamless operation of supply chains, supporting businesses in achieving their strategic goals.

2. Importance of Logistics and Distribution in Modern Business

In an increasingly interconnected global economy, logistics and distribution management have become critical to competitive advantage. Their significance can be analyzed through various lenses:

2.1 Operational Efficiency

Efficient logistics reduce delays, minimize waste, and optimize resource utilization. By streamlining transportation, warehousing, and inventory management, companies can lower operational costs while maintaining service quality.

Example: Just-in-Time (JIT) logistics minimizes inventory levels by delivering materials precisely when needed, reducing storage costs and enhancing efficiency.

2.2 Enhancing Customer Satisfaction

Modern customers demand faster delivery, accurate tracking, and flexible return options. Superior logistics ensure timely deliveries and enhance the overall customer experience, fostering loyalty and trust.

Example: E-commerce giants like Amazon use advanced distribution networks to offer next-day or same-day delivery, setting industry benchmarks for customer service.

2.3 Strategic Advantage

In a competitive marketplace, robust logistics systems enable businesses to expand into new markets and adapt to fluctuating demand. Distribution channels serve as a critical link between manufacturers and consumers, ensuring product availability in diverse regions.

Example: Global companies like Coca-Cola rely on highly localized distribution networks to maintain a consistent presence in over 200 countries.

2.4 Risk Mitigation

Effective logistics mitigate risks associated with supply chain disruptions, such as natural disasters, labor strikes, or geopolitical instability. Proactive planning and contingency strategies enhance resilience.

Case in Point: During the COVID-19 pandemic, companies with agile logistics systems were better equipped to manage disruptions and meet increased demand for essential goods.

2.5 Supporting Global Trade

Logistics is a cornerstone of international trade, facilitating the movement of goods across borders. Efficient management ensures compliance with trade regulations, reduces customs delays, and minimizes costs.

3. Evolution of Logistics and Distribution Management

The history of logistics and distribution reflects a journey from basic transportation methods to complex, technology-driven systems. Analyzing its evolution provides insights into its transformation and future trajectory.

3.1 Early Beginnings: Pre-Industrial Era

Logistics originated in military operations, where the movement of troops, supplies, and equipment was critical to success.

Ancient trade routes, such as the Silk Road, exemplify early distribution networks, enabling the exchange of goods across continents.

3.2 Industrial Revolution (18th-19th Century)

The advent of mechanization and mass production revolutionized logistics. Factories required efficient transportation to move raw materials and distribute finished products.

Railroads and steamships emerged as key transportation modes, reducing transit times and expanding market reach.

Warehousing systems became more structured to support large-scale production and distribution.

3.3 The Rise of Global Trade (20th Century)

Post-World War II economic growth spurred international trade, necessitating more sophisticated logistics systems.

The invention of standardized shipping containers in the 1950s transformed freight transport, enabling intermodal logistics (seamless transfer between ships, trains, and trucks).

Advances in air transportation shortened delivery times for high-value and perishable goods.

3.4 The Technology Era (Late 20th Century - Early 21st Century)

Computerization and the advent of Enterprise Resource Planning (ERP) systems enhanced the coordination of logistics operations.

Real-time tracking and data analytics improved decision-making and demand forecasting.

E-commerce introduced new challenges and opportunities, requiring companies to build agile and responsive logistics networks.

3.5 The Digital Transformation Era (Present Day)

Automation and Robotics: Warehouse automation systems and autonomous vehicles optimize efficiency and reduce labor costs.

Internet of Things (IoT): IoT devices provide real-time data on inventory levels, shipment locations, and environmental conditions.

Sustainability: A growing focus on green logistics emphasizes reducing carbon footprints through renewable energy, electric vehicles, and sustainable packaging.

3.6 Future Trends in Logistics

The future of logistics is being shaped by emerging technologies and changing consumer expectations. Anticipated trends include:

Artificial Intelligence (AI): Advanced AI systems will improve routing, forecasting, and customer interactions.

Blockchain: Secure and transparent transaction records will revolutionize supply chain management.

Hyperloop and Drone Delivery: Cutting-edge transportation technologies promise faster and more efficient delivery systems.

Logistics and distribution management have evolved from rudimentary transportation methods to intricate, technology-driven systems that are integral to modern business success. Their scope encompasses transportation, warehousing, inventory, and customer service, while their importance lies in operational efficiency, customer satisfaction, and strategic advantage. The historical evolution of logistics highlights the adaptive nature of the field, driven by innovation and the changing demands of global trade. As businesses navigate the complexities of today's marketplace, logistics and distribution remain indispensable in achieving efficiency, resilience, and growth.

The Role of Logistics in the Supply Chain

Logistics serves as the backbone of supply chain management, ensuring the efficient movement and storage of goods, services, and information throughout the supply chain. This chapter explores the distinctions and connections between logistics and supply chain management, the integration of logistics with supply chain processes, and the ways logistics contributes to value creation for businesses and their customers.

1. Logistics vs. Supply Chain Management

Understanding the relationship and differences between logistics and supply chain management (SCM) is fundamental to appreciating their roles in business operations.

1.1 Defining Logistics and Supply Chain Management

Logistics focuses on the operational aspect of moving and storing goods, ensuring that they are delivered to the right place, at the right time, in the right condition, and at the right cost.

Key Activities: Transportation, warehousing, inventory management, order fulfillment, and reverse logistics.

Supply Chain Management encompasses a broader scope, involving the strategic coordination of end-to-end processes that deliver goods and services to customers.

Key Activities: Sourcing, procurement, production, logistics, and demand planning.

1.2 Differences Between Logistics and Supply Chain Management

Aspect	Logistics	Supply Chain Management
Scope	Operational focus	Strategic, end-to-end focus
Objective	Efficient movement and storage	Integration and optimization of processes
Key Players	Carriers, warehouse operators	Suppliers, manufacturers, distributors, retailers
Decision Level	Tactical	Strategic and operational

1.3 Interconnection Between Logistics and SCM

While logistics is a component of SCM, it plays a crucial role in executing the strategies developed within the supply chain. SCM relies on logistics to ensure seamless operations, while logistics benefits from the overarching framework and planning provided by SCM.

2. Integration with Supply Chain Processes

Logistics must be integrated into supply chain processes to achieve overall efficiency and effectiveness. This integration involves synchronizing logistics activities with sourcing, production, and delivery.

2.1 Key Areas of Integration

Procurement and Inbound Logistics

Coordinating the transportation and storage of raw materials from suppliers to production facilities.

Example: Automotive manufacturers rely on just-in-time deliveries to keep production lines running smoothly.

Production and Internal Logistics

Ensuring materials and components are available for uninterrupted production processes.

Integration reduces downtime and aligns production schedules with logistics capabilities.

Outbound Logistics and Distribution

Managing the movement of finished goods from production facilities to customers.

Example: Consumer electronics companies use centralized warehouses to meet global demand efficiently.

Reverse Logistics

Handling product returns, recycling, and disposal.

Example: E-commerce companies streamline returns processes to maintain customer satisfaction.

2.2 Benefits of Integration

Improved Visibility: Real-time data sharing between logistics and other supply chain functions enhances decision-making.

Cost Optimization: Integrated planning reduces redundant activities and optimizes resource allocation.

Customer-Centric Approach: Synchronization ensures timely deliveries and better responsiveness to customer demands.

2.3 Tools and Technologies for Integration

Enterprise Resource Planning (ERP) Systems: Unify logistics and SCM data for streamlined operations.

Transportation Management Systems (TMS): Optimize route planning and freight management.

Internet of Things (IoT): Enable real-time tracking and monitoring of shipments.

3. Value Creation Through Logistics

Logistics creates value by enhancing efficiency, improving customer satisfaction, and supporting business growth. Its role extends beyond operational tasks to become a strategic enabler of competitive advantage.

3.1 Operational Efficiency

Efficient logistics reduce costs, minimize waste, and improve resource utilization. By optimizing transportation, inventory management, and warehousing, businesses achieve leaner operations.

Example: Companies like Walmart use cross-docking to eliminate unnecessary storage, reducing lead times and costs.

3.2 Enhancing Customer Satisfaction

Logistics ensures that products are delivered accurately and on time, meeting or exceeding customer expectations. This reliability fosters trust and loyalty.

Example: Companies offering same-day or next-day delivery leverage logistics excellence to differentiate themselves in competitive markets.

3.3 Facilitating Market Expansion

Through robust logistics networks, businesses can enter new markets and reach a global audience. Effective distribution systems ensure product availability across diverse geographies.

Case in Point: Apple's global logistics network supports the simultaneous launch of products in multiple countries.

3.4 Enabling Sustainability

Modern logistics incorporates green practices to reduce environmental impact, such as route optimization, fuel-efficient vehicles, and sustainable packaging.

Example: DHL's GoGreen program aims to achieve zero-emissions logistics through renewable energy and alternative fuel technologies.

3.5 Supporting Innovation

Logistics innovation enables businesses to adapt to changing market demands, such as the rise of e-commerce or the need for cold chain logistics in pharmaceuticals.

Emerging Trend: Companies are using drones for last-mile delivery to improve speed and reduce costs in urban areas.

Logistics plays a central role in the supply chain by connecting suppliers, manufacturers, distributors, and customers. Its integration with supply chain processes ensures seamless operations, while its efficiency and adaptability create significant value for businesses. By understanding the distinctions between logistics and SCM, leveraging integration tools, and focusing on value creation, businesses can achieve operational excellence and sustain competitive advantages in today's dynamic marketplace.

Key Concepts in Distribution Management

Distribution management is an essential component of supply chain operations, ensuring that products move efficiently from manufacturers to end customers. This chapter explores distribution channels and networks, the functions of distribution, and the trends and challenges shaping modern distribution.

1. Distribution Channels and Networks

Distribution channels and networks define the pathways through which goods flow from producers to consumers. Understanding these structures is critical for optimizing delivery efficiency and customer satisfaction.

1.1 Distribution Channels

A distribution channel refers to the route a product takes from the manufacturer to the final consumer. The complexity of this route depends on the number of intermediaries involved.

Direct Channel: The manufacturer sells directly to the consumer without intermediaries.

Example: E-commerce businesses like Tesla's direct sales model.

Indirect Channel: Includes intermediaries such as wholesalers, retailers, or distributors.

Example: FMCG companies like Procter & Gamble using a network of wholesalers and retailers.

Levels of Distribution Channels:

Zero-Level (Direct): Manufacturer → Consumer

One-Level: Manufacturer → Retailer → Consumer

Two-Level: Manufacturer → Wholesaler → Retailer → Consumer

Three-Level or More: Incorporates additional intermediaries like agents or brokers.

1.2 Distribution Networks

A distribution network is the system of interconnected locations and entities that facilitate product movement. It includes warehouses, distribution centers, and transportation routes.

Centralized Networks: Few distribution hubs, typically used by companies prioritizing cost-efficiency.

Decentralized Networks: Multiple distribution points closer to customers, used for faster delivery.

Hybrid Networks: Combine centralized and decentralized models for balance.

1.3 Factors Influencing Channel Design

Nature of the Product: Perishables require shorter channels, while durable goods can tolerate longer ones.

Market Characteristics: Geographic spread and customer preferences shape channel choices.

Company Goals: Cost reduction, brand control, or customer reach.

Technology: Innovations like digital platforms enable direct-to-consumer channels.

2. Functions of Distribution

Distribution is not merely about moving products but involves several functions that ensure smooth operations and customer satisfaction.

2.1 Transportation

Moves goods between production sites, warehouses, and customers.

Efficient transportation minimizes delays and reduces costs.

Modal options include road, rail, air, and sea, chosen based on cost, speed, and product type.

2.2 Warehousing and Storage

Provides a space for inventory between production and delivery.

Warehouses optimize order fulfillment and buffer against demand fluctuations.

2.3 Inventory Management

Ensures the right stock levels to meet demand without overstocking.

Techniques like Just-in-Time (JIT) and ABC Analysis improve efficiency.

2.4 Order Processing and Fulfillment

Involves receiving, verifying, and dispatching customer orders.

Technology like Warehouse Management Systems (WMS) streamlines these operations.

2.5 Customer Service

Distribution supports customer satisfaction through accurate deliveries, on-time shipping, and responsive issue resolution.

2.6 Market Feedback and Reverse Logistics

Distribution channels act as feedback loops, gathering data on customer preferences.

Reverse logistics, such as returns or recycling, enhances customer trust and sustainability efforts.

3. Trends and Challenges in Distribution

Modern distribution is undergoing significant transformations, driven by technology, customer expectations, and market dynamics.

3.1 Key Trends in Distribution

E-Commerce and Omnichannel Distribution

The rise of online shopping demands flexible distribution systems.

Omnichannel strategies integrate online and offline channels for seamless customer experiences.

Last-Mile Delivery Innovations

Companies are investing in drones, autonomous vehicles, and crowd-sourced delivery models.

Example: Amazon's drone-based Prime Air delivery initiative.

Sustainability in Distribution

Focus on reducing carbon footprints through fuel-efficient vehicles, optimized routes, and green packaging.

Example: Companies like UPS and DHL adopting electric delivery vehicles.

Automation and Robotics

Automated warehouses and robotic picking systems improve speed and accuracy.

Example: Amazon's robotic fulfillment centers.

Data-Driven Distribution

Advanced analytics and IoT sensors provide real-time visibility into inventory and shipments.

3.2 Challenges in Distribution

Rising Customer Expectations

Customers expect faster delivery times, tracking visibility, and flexible return options.

Adapting to these demands requires significant investments in technology and infrastructure.

Cost Pressures

Balancing cost efficiency with service quality is a constant challenge.

Fluctuations in fuel prices and labor costs further complicate cost management.

Globalization and Localization

Managing global supply chains requires navigating complex regulations, tariffs, and logistics constraints.

Simultaneously, meeting local market demands necessitates tailored strategies.

Technological Disruptions

Rapid technological changes make it difficult for companies to keep up without substantial investments.

Risk Management

Distribution systems face risks from natural disasters, geopolitical instability, and cyber-attacks.

Building resilient networks and contingency plans is essential.

Distribution management is a critical function in the supply chain, encompassing the design of channels, performance of essential functions, and adaptation to evolving trends. Effective distribution channels and networks ensure goods flow efficiently, while the core functions of transportation, inventory, and customer service drive operational success. However, businesses must navigate trends like e-commerce, automation, and sustainability while overcoming challenges like cost pressures and risk management. By embracing innovation and aligning distribution strategies with customer needs, companies can maintain competitiveness in an increasingly complex marketplace.

Strategic Logistics Planning

Strategic logistics planning is essential for aligning logistics functions with corporate objectives, ensuring efficient resource utilization, and achieving long-term competitiveness. This chapter delves into logistics strategy and its alignment with corporate goals, the importance of strategic decision-making in logistics, and tools and methods for long-term planning.

1. Logistics Strategy and Alignment with Corporate Goals

A well-formulated logistics strategy bridges the gap between operational efficiency and organizational vision. This alignment ensures logistics activities support broader corporate goals.

1.1 Defining Logistics Strategy

A logistics strategy encompasses plans and actions aimed at optimizing the flow of goods, services, and information. It addresses key areas like transportation, warehousing, inventory management, and customer service.

Types of Logistics Strategies:

Cost Leadership Strategy: Focuses on minimizing costs through operational efficiencies.

Example: Walmart's logistics network emphasizes cost reduction via centralized distribution and cross-docking.

Differentiation Strategy: Prioritizes high-quality services, such as faster delivery or enhanced tracking.

Example: FedEx's overnight delivery model.

Focus Strategy: Tailors logistics operations to specific market segments or geographic regions.

1.2 Alignment with Corporate Goals

Logistics strategy must align with corporate goals to create a unified direction for the organization.

Key Elements of Alignment:

Customer-Centric Approach: Ensuring logistics supports superior customer experiences.

Sustainability Goals: Implementing eco-friendly practices in line with corporate environmental commitments.

Profitability Objectives: Balancing cost efficiency with revenue generation through optimized logistics.

Case Example: Amazon aligns its logistics strategy with its goal of becoming the most customer-centric company by offering rapid delivery options through its Prime service.

1.3 Benefits of Alignment:

Consistency Across Operations: Ensures logistics decisions are in harmony with organizational priorities.

Enhanced Competitiveness: Logistics becomes a strategic enabler rather than just a support function.

Risk Mitigation: Strategic alignment helps preempt disruptions that could derail corporate objectives.

2. Importance of Strategic Decisions in Logistics

Strategic decision-making in logistics ensures that long-term goals are met while addressing dynamic market conditions and operational complexities.

2.1 Key Areas Requiring Strategic Decisions:

Facility Location and Network Design:

Deciding where to establish warehouses, distribution centers, and transportation hubs.

Example: Global companies like Nike strategically place distribution centers near major markets to reduce lead times.

Technology Adoption:

Choosing the right technologies, such as Warehouse Management Systems (WMS) or Transportation Management Systems (TMS), to enhance logistics efficiency.

Outsourcing vs. In-House Operations:

Strategic choice between using third-party logistics providers (3PLs) or managing logistics internally.

Example: Many companies outsource last-mile delivery to firms like UPS or DHL.

Sustainability Initiatives:

Decisions on adopting green logistics practices, such as using electric vehicles or optimizing routes for lower emissions.

2.2 Factors Influencing Strategic Decisions:

Market Trends: E-commerce growth demands faster delivery and expanded networks.

Regulatory Environment: Compliance with trade laws, safety standards, and environmental regulations.

Customer Expectations: Increasing demand for transparency, speed, and flexibility.

Cost Considerations: Balancing investment in infrastructure and technology with long-term benefits.

2.3 Impact of Strategic Decisions:

Enhanced Efficiency: Improves overall supply chain performance.

Resilience: Builds adaptability to withstand disruptions, such as economic downturns or natural disasters.

Customer Loyalty: Ensures reliable, high-quality service, fostering repeat business.

3. Long-Term Planning Tools and Methods

Strategic logistics planning involves using specific tools and methodologies to forecast, analyze, and optimize operations for the future.

3.1 Forecasting and Demand Planning Tools:

Historical Data Analysis: Using past sales and shipment data to predict future demand.

Machine Learning Models: Leveraging AI for dynamic and accurate demand forecasting.

Scenario Analysis: Evaluating the impact of various market conditions on logistics operations.

Example: Companies simulate high-demand scenarios during holidays to prepare their logistics networks.

3.2 Network Optimization Models:

Linear Programming: Optimizes routes, facility locations, and inventory levels for cost efficiency.

Simulation Software: Tests different logistics strategies to identify the most effective approach.

3.3 Strategic Planning Frameworks:

SWOT Analysis (Strengths, Weaknesses, Opportunities, Threats): Assesses internal and external factors influencing logistics.

Example: A company may leverage strengths like a robust transportation fleet while addressing weaknesses in warehouse capacity.

Balanced Scorecard: Aligns logistics metrics with organizational goals, tracking performance across cost, service, and sustainability.

3.4 Collaboration Tools:

Integrated Supply Chain Platforms: Facilitate real-time data sharing between stakeholders.

Blockchain Technology: Enhances transparency and traceability in logistics.

3.5 Risk Management Methods:

Risk Matrices: Identify and prioritize risks based on likelihood and impact.

Contingency Planning: Develop backup strategies for potential disruptions, such as alternative suppliers or routes.

Strategic logistics planning is a cornerstone of effective supply chain management, enabling organizations to align logistics with corporate objectives, make informed long-term decisions, and utilize advanced tools for optimization. By focusing on strategic alignment, businesses can transform logistics from a cost center into a source of competitive advantage. Embracing robust planning tools, staying attuned to market dynamics, and adopting innovative solutions will ensure logistics remains a driving force in achieving organizational success.

Section 2: Core Components of Logistics and Distribution

Transportation Management

Transportation management is a pivotal element of logistics and distribution, involving the planning, execution, and optimization of the movement of goods. This chapter explores modes of transportation, criteria for selecting the right mode for business needs, and strategies for cost management in transportation.

1. Modes of Transportation

Transportation modes determine how goods are moved from one location to another. Each mode has unique characteristics, advantages, and limitations, influencing its suitability for specific logistics needs.

1.1 Road Transportation

Road transport is one of the most versatile and widely used modes, offering flexibility in routing and delivery.

Advantages:

Ideal for short and medium distances.

Door-to-door delivery capability.

Minimal handling reduces the risk of product damage.

Challenges:

Vulnerable to traffic congestion and weather disruptions.

Higher costs for long-distance hauls compared to rail or sea.

Use Cases:

Distribution of consumer goods within urban areas.

Transportation of perishable items requiring quick delivery.

1.2 Rail Transportation

Rail is a cost-effective option for transporting bulk goods over long distances.

Advantages:

High capacity for heavy or voluminous shipments.

Fuel efficiency and lower environmental impact compared to road transport.

Reliable schedules unaffected by road traffic.

Challenges:

Limited flexibility in destination access.

Additional costs for last-mile delivery using other modes.

Use Cases:

Transporting raw materials like coal, steel, or grain.

Moving large consignments to central hubs for further distribution.

1.3 Air Transportation

Air transport is the fastest mode, suitable for high-value or time-sensitive shipments.

Advantages:

Rapid delivery over long distances.

Ideal for international trade and emergency logistics.

High security for valuable goods.

Challenges:

High costs compared to other modes.

Weight and size limitations for cargo.

Use Cases:

Transportation of electronics, pharmaceuticals, or luxury goods.

Emergency shipments like medical supplies.

1.4 Sea Transportation

Sea transport is the most economical mode for moving large volumes over international distances.

Advantages:

Cost-effective for bulk shipments.

Suitable for heavy, oversized, or hazardous cargo.

A cornerstone of global trade.

Challenges:

Slow transit times.

Susceptibility to weather conditions and port congestion.

Use Cases:

Transporting oil, chemicals, or machinery.

Import and export of goods like automobiles or apparel.

1.5 Multimodal Transportation

Combines two or more modes (e.g., rail and road) to optimize cost and efficiency.

Advantages:

Flexibility in addressing complex logistics needs.

Reduces transit times compared to relying on a single mode.

Challenges:

Coordination complexity between modes.

Potential delays at intermodal transfer points.

2. Selecting the Right Mode for Your Business

Choosing the appropriate mode of transportation is critical for cost-efficiency, timely delivery, and customer satisfaction. The selection process should consider the following factors:

2.1 Nature of the Goods:

Perishable Goods: Require fast modes like road or air to ensure freshness.

Bulk or Heavy Cargo: Rail or sea is often more economical.

2.2 Distance and Destination:

Short distances favor road transport, while long-haul routes often benefit from rail or sea.

Remote or international destinations may necessitate air transport.

2.3 Cost Considerations:

Businesses must balance freight costs against the value and urgency of the shipment.

Example: High-value goods may justify the expense of air transport.

2.4 Speed Requirements:

Urgent deliveries require faster modes like air or express road services.

Non-urgent shipments can leverage slower, cost-effective modes like sea or rail.

2.5 Environmental Impact:

Companies focused on sustainability may prioritize greener options like rail or hybrid transport systems.

2.6 Infrastructure and Accessibility:

Availability of road networks, rail lines, ports, and airports near the source and destination influences mode selection.

2.7 Reliability and Security:

High-value or fragile goods require secure and reliable modes, such as air transport or dedicated freight services.

3. Cost Management in Transportation

Transportation is one of the largest components of logistics costs, making effective cost management crucial for profitability.

3.1 Optimizing Route Planning:

Use route optimization software to reduce mileage and fuel consumption.

Example: UPS minimizes left-hand turns to save fuel and time.

3.2 Consolidating Shipments:

Combining smaller shipments into a single load reduces costs per unit.

Example: LTL (Less-than-Truckload) services allow multiple companies to share transport costs.

3.3 Negotiating Freight Rates:

Establish long-term contracts with carriers to lock in favorable rates.

Use freight marketplaces to compare rates and find competitive options.

3.4 Leveraging Technology:

Implement Transportation Management Systems (TMS) for real-time tracking and efficient load planning.

IoT sensors in vehicles provide data for monitoring fuel usage and vehicle performance.

3.5 Adopting Multimodal Strategies:

Optimize cost and efficiency by integrating different transport modes.

Example: Use rail for the long haul and road for last-mile delivery.

3.6 Managing Fuel Costs:

Invest in fuel-efficient vehicles or explore alternative energy sources like electric trucks.

Implement driver training programs to encourage fuel-saving practices.

3.7 Reducing Empty Miles:

Match backhaul loads to avoid running empty vehicles on return trips.

Example: Freight matching platforms connect shippers with available capacity.

3.8 Monitoring and Analyzing Performance:

Use key performance indicators (KPIs) such as cost per mile, on-time delivery rate, and load utilization to track efficiency and identify cost-saving opportunities.

Transportation management is a critical pillar of logistics and distribution, encompassing decisions on modes of transportation, selection criteria, and cost control. By understanding the strengths and limitations of each transport mode, businesses can tailor solutions to meet specific needs. Strategic selection of transportation modes, combined with advanced cost management practices, ensures efficient movement of goods while maintaining profitability and service quality. As technological advancements continue to reshape the logistics landscape, businesses must remain agile and proactive in optimizing transportation strategies.

Warehousing and Storage

Warehousing and storage are fundamental components of logistics and supply chain management. They serve as hubs for storing, managing, and distributing goods efficiently. This chapter delves into the functions of a warehouse, explores types of warehouses, and outlines the key considerations in warehouse design and operations to optimize storage and distribution processes.

1. Functions of a Warehouse

Warehouses play a critical role in ensuring a seamless flow of goods across the supply chain. Their functions extend beyond storage, contributing to operational efficiency and customer satisfaction.

1.1 Storage of Goods

The primary function of a warehouse is to store goods for a specified duration until they are required.

Temporary Storage: Goods are held temporarily before being distributed to retailers or end-users.

Seasonal Storage: Warehouses store products produced or purchased in bulk for future sales, such as agricultural produce or holiday merchandise.

1.2 Consolidation and Break-Bulk

Warehouses facilitate the consolidation of goods from various suppliers and the breakdown of large shipments into smaller ones for distribution.

Consolidation: Combines shipments from different sources to reduce transportation costs.

Break-Bulk: Large shipments are divided into smaller lots for delivery to individual locations.

1.3 Order Fulfillment

Modern warehouses function as order-fulfillment centers, picking, packing, and preparing goods for shipment.

E-commerce Integration: Warehouses process individual orders efficiently, critical for online retailers.

Accuracy and Speed: Advanced systems ensure timely and accurate order processing.

1.4 Inventory Management

Warehouses monitor and control inventory levels, ensuring adequate stock availability while minimizing overstocking.

Tracking: Use of inventory management systems for real-time tracking of stock levels.

Optimization: Ensures that the right products are available at the right time and location.

1.5 Value-Added Services

Warehouses often provide additional services to enhance product readiness.

Packaging: Goods are repackaged or labeled as per customer requirements.

Assembly: Products are assembled or kitted before shipment.

Quality Control: Inspection and testing of goods to ensure compliance with quality standards.

1.6 Risk Mitigation

Warehouses protect goods from risks such as theft, damage, or spoilage.

Security Measures: CCTV, access control systems, and regular audits safeguard against theft.

Environmental Controls: Temperature and humidity regulation prevent spoilage of sensitive goods like food or pharmaceuticals.

2. Types of Warehouses

Warehouses come in various forms, tailored to meet specific business needs and operational requirements. Below are some common types:

2.1 Private Warehouses

Owned and operated by businesses to store their goods.

Advantages: Full control over operations, custom-designed facilities.

Disadvantages: High initial investment and operational costs.

Use Cases: Large manufacturers, retailers, and e-commerce companies.

2.2 Public Warehouses

Available for use by multiple businesses on a rental basis.

Advantages: Low initial cost, flexibility in terms of space and duration.

Disadvantages: Limited control over operations and shared facilities.

Use Cases: Small businesses or companies with seasonal storage needs.

2.3 Bonded Warehouses

Used to store imported goods under customs supervision until duties are paid.

Advantages: Delays duty payments until goods are released for sale.

Disadvantages: Limited to specific use cases.

Use Cases: Importers and exporters.

2.4 Automated Warehouses

Highly advanced facilities with automation technologies like robotics, conveyors, and automated storage and retrieval systems (AS/RS).

Advantages: Increased efficiency, reduced labor costs, and high accuracy.

Disadvantages: Significant initial investment.

Use Cases: E-commerce and high-volume businesses.

2.5 Cold Storage Warehouses

Specialized warehouses for perishable goods like food, pharmaceuticals, and chemicals.

Advantages: Maintain product integrity through temperature control.

Disadvantages: Higher operational costs due to energy requirements.

Use Cases: Food industry, biotech, and healthcare.

2.6 Distribution Centers

Focus on rapid movement of goods rather than long-term storage.

Advantages: Enable same-day or next-day delivery services.

Disadvantages: Limited storage capacity.

Use Cases: Retailers and e-commerce.

3. Key Considerations in Warehouse Design and Operations

An effective warehouse design and operation strategy enhances efficiency, reduces costs, and meets business goals.

3.1 Location and Accessibility

Selecting the right location impacts transportation costs, delivery times, and customer satisfaction.

Proximity to Customers: Reduces transit times and costs.

Infrastructure: Availability of roads, railways, ports, and airports.

Regulations: Compliance with zoning laws and environmental standards.

3.2 Layout Design

An efficient warehouse layout maximizes space utilization and workflow.

Space Utilization: Optimal use of vertical and horizontal space.

Flow Optimization: Ensure a smooth flow of goods from receiving to shipping.

Zoning: Segregation of areas for storage, packing, and quality control.

3.3 Technology Integration

Modern warehouses rely on technology to enhance efficiency and accuracy.

Warehouse Management Systems (WMS): Real-time tracking and inventory management.

Automation: Use of robotics and conveyors for faster operations.

IoT Sensors: Monitor environmental conditions like temperature and humidity.

3.4 Safety and Compliance

Safety protocols ensure a secure working environment for employees and goods.

Hazard Prevention: Fire suppression systems, spill containment, and ergonomic practices.

Regulatory Compliance: Adherence to OSHA and other safety standards.

Training: Regular training for employees on safety procedures.

3.5 Scalability and Flexibility

Designing for scalability ensures that the warehouse can grow with business needs.

Modular Design: Facilities that can expand or adapt to changing requirements.

Flexible Operations: Ability to handle varying volumes and product types.

3.6 Sustainability Initiatives

Eco-friendly practices reduce the environmental impact and align with corporate sustainability goals.

Energy Efficiency: LED lighting and renewable energy sources like solar panels.

Waste Management: Recycling programs and minimizing packaging waste.

Green Certifications: Achieving certifications like LEED for sustainable design.

Warehousing and storage form the backbone of efficient supply chain operations. From their multifaceted functions to the diverse types tailored to specific needs, warehouses ensure goods are stored, managed, and distributed effectively. Designing and operating warehouses requires careful attention to factors such as location, layout, technology, safety, and sustainability. As businesses adapt to evolving customer demands and technological advancements, warehouses must continue to innovate to remain integral to supply chain success.

Inventory Management

Effective inventory management is a cornerstone of logistics and supply chain operations. It ensures that the right quantity of goods is available at the right time, balancing customer demand with operational efficiency. This chapter explores the importance of inventory in logistics, examines various inventory management techniques, and discusses strategies for balancing costs and service levels.

1. Importance of Inventory in Logistics

Inventory acts as a buffer between supply and demand, ensuring smooth operations in logistics and the supply chain. Its significance extends beyond mere storage, influencing cost efficiency, customer satisfaction, and overall business performance.

1.1 Meeting Customer Demand

One of the primary reasons for maintaining inventory is to meet customer expectations for timely delivery.

Product Availability: Ensures customers receive the goods they need without delays.

Avoiding Stockouts: Reduces the risk of losing customers to competitors due to unavailability of products.

1.2 Managing Supply Chain Disruptions

Inventory serves as a safeguard against uncertainties in supply or demand.

Supply Delays: Acts as a buffer when suppliers experience production or delivery delays.

Demand Fluctuations: Absorbs sudden spikes in customer demand, especially during peak seasons or promotions.

1.3 Economies of Scale

Maintaining inventory allows businesses to benefit from economies of scale.

Bulk Purchasing: Companies can order in larger quantities to negotiate better prices and reduce per-unit costs.

Efficient Production: Ensures continuous production without interruptions caused by material shortages.

1.4 Optimizing Transportation and Storage

Strategic inventory placement can minimize transportation and storage costs.

Reduced Freight Costs: Consolidating shipments reduces transportation expenses.

Efficient Distribution: Storing inventory closer to demand centers reduces last-mile delivery costs.

1.5 Enhancing Operational Efficiency

Proper inventory levels support smooth workflow and reduce inefficiencies.

Production Continuity: Prevents halts in manufacturing due to raw material shortages.

Improved Planning: Accurate inventory data aids in better production and procurement planning.

2. Inventory Management Techniques

Effective inventory management involves selecting the right strategies and techniques to control stock levels and reduce waste while maintaining service quality.

2.1 Economic Order Quantity (EOQ)

EOQ is a mathematical model that determines the ideal order quantity to minimize total inventory costs.

Order Costs: Balances the cost of placing orders with the cost of holding inventory.

Application: Best for businesses with consistent demand and predictable supply cycles.

2.2 ABC Analysis

This technique categorizes inventory into three groups based on value and importance.

A Items: High-value items with low frequency of use; require tight control.

B Items: Moderate-value items with moderate usage.

C Items: Low-value items with high frequency of use; require less stringent controls.

2.3 Just-in-Time (JIT)

JIT aims to minimize inventory by receiving goods only when needed.

Advantages: Reduces carrying costs and waste.

Challenges: Requires reliable suppliers and precise demand forecasting.

2.4 Safety Stock

Maintaining a buffer stock to protect against uncertainties in supply or demand.

Calculation: Based on historical demand variability and lead times.

Benefits: Minimizes risk of stockouts while maintaining service levels.

2.5 Inventory Turnover Ratio

This metric measures how often inventory is sold and replaced over a period.

High Turnover: Indicates efficient inventory use and strong sales.

Low Turnover: Suggests overstocking or slow-moving products.

2.6 Perpetual Inventory System

Tracks inventory levels in real time using technology.

Automation: Uses barcodes, RFID, and inventory management software.

Accuracy: Reduces manual errors and provides instant visibility into stock levels.

2.7 Vendor-Managed Inventory (VMI)

In VMI, suppliers manage inventory levels on behalf of the business.

Benefits: Reduces stockouts and administrative burdens.

Requirements: Strong collaboration and data sharing with suppliers.

3. Balancing Costs and Service Levels

Balancing inventory costs and service levels is critical for achieving operational and financial objectives.

3.1 Understanding Costs

Inventory management involves two primary cost components:

Carrying Costs: Expenses related to storing and maintaining inventory, including warehousing, insurance, depreciation, and obsolescence.

Stockout Costs: Loss of revenue and customer goodwill due to unavailability of products.

3.2 Determining Optimal Inventory Levels

The key to balancing costs and service levels lies in maintaining optimal inventory levels.

Reorder Points: Set inventory levels at which new orders are triggered to avoid stockouts.

Demand Forecasting: Use historical data and predictive analytics to anticipate demand accurately.

3.3 Inventory Optimization Tools

Technology plays a significant role in optimizing inventory and balancing trade-offs.

Inventory Management Software: Provides real-time data on stock levels, demand trends, and lead times.

AI and Machine Learning: Enhances demand forecasting accuracy and identifies inventory inefficiencies.

3.4 Service Level Agreements (SLAs)

Define acceptable service levels for inventory availability and delivery performance.

Measurement: Monitor fill rates, on-time deliveries, and order accuracy.

Adjustments: Align inventory policies to meet SLA requirements without overstocking.

3.5 Lean Inventory Management

Adopting lean principles helps reduce waste while maintaining service quality.

Focus on Value: Stock only what is necessary to meet customer needs.

Continuous Improvement: Regularly review inventory processes for potential improvements.

Inventory management is a balancing act that requires strategic planning, effective techniques, and continuous monitoring. Its role in logistics extends beyond storage, directly influencing cost efficiency, customer satisfaction, and operational success. By adopting appropriate inventory management techniques and aligning costs with service levels, businesses can achieve an agile and responsive supply chain capable of thriving in today's competitive marketplace.

Order Fulfillment and Customer Service

Order fulfillment is the backbone of logistics operations, bridging the gap between customer expectations and business performance. It involves the entire process of receiving, processing, and delivering orders. This chapter delves into the order processing workflow, strategies for ensuring customer satisfaction, and the role of technology in order fulfillment.

1. Order Processing Workflow

The order processing workflow is a systematic approach to managing customer orders, ensuring accuracy, efficiency, and timely delivery.

1.1 Steps in the Order Processing Workflow

Order Placement:

Customers place orders through various channels, such as online platforms, phone calls, or physical stores.

Accuracy at this stage ensures the right products, quantities, and delivery instructions are captured.

Order Verification:

The business confirms the order details, checks inventory availability, and verifies payment.

Automated systems often handle this stage to reduce manual errors.

Inventory Allocation:

The system allocates inventory to the order based on stock levels and warehouse locations.

Advanced algorithms optimize inventory allocation to minimize delivery times.

Order Picking:

Warehouse staff or automated systems retrieve items from storage based on the order details.

Efficient picking strategies, such as batch picking or zone picking, can improve speed and accuracy.

Order Packing:

Items are packed securely to prevent damage during transit.

Sustainable packaging materials are increasingly used to align with environmental goals.

Shipping:

Orders are assigned to carriers, and delivery schedules are finalized.

Tracking numbers are generated and shared with customers.

Delivery and Confirmation:

The carrier delivers the order to the customer.

Proof of delivery is collected to confirm completion.

1.2 Key Metrics for Order Processing

Order Cycle Time: Measures the time from order placement to delivery.

Order Accuracy Rate: Percentage of orders delivered without errors.

Fill Rate: Percentage of orders fulfilled from available inventory.

2. Ensuring Customer Satisfaction

Customer satisfaction in order fulfillment is critical for retaining loyalty and driving repeat business. Effective strategies focus on minimizing errors, improving communication, and delivering value.

2.1 Timely Delivery

On-Time Performance: Delivering orders as promised is vital for customer trust.

Real-Time Tracking: Providing customers with updates on their order status enhances transparency.

2.2 Accuracy in Fulfillment

Error-Free Deliveries: Ensuring the correct items and quantities are delivered.

Returns and Replacements: Streamlining processes for handling incorrect or damaged products.

2.3 Personalized Service

Customized Packaging: Adding a personal touch, such as thank-you notes or tailored packaging, can enhance the customer experience.

Flexible Delivery Options: Offering choices like expedited shipping or delivery windows caters to customer preferences.

2.4 Proactive Communication

Order Updates: Sending notifications at each stage of the fulfillment process.

Customer Support: Providing responsive and accessible support channels for inquiries and issues.

2.5 Measuring Customer Satisfaction

Net Promoter Score (NPS): Gauges customer willingness to recommend the business.

Customer Feedback: Collecting and analyzing feedback to identify areas for improvement.

3. Technology in Order Fulfillment

Technology has revolutionized order fulfillment, enabling businesses to enhance efficiency, reduce errors, and improve customer experiences.

3.1 Automation in Order Processing

Order Management Systems (OMS): Automates order capturing, verification, and processing.

Warehouse Management Systems (WMS): Coordinates picking, packing, and shipping activities.

3.2 Robotics and AI

Automated Picking Systems: Robots can locate and pick items with high precision.

AI-Driven Analytics: Predictive analytics optimize inventory allocation and order routing.

3.3 Real-Time Tracking and Visibility

GPS and IoT Devices: Provide real-time updates on the location and status of shipments.

Customer Portals: Allow customers to track their orders and access delivery information.

3.4 E-Commerce Integration

Omnichannel Fulfillment: Integrates online and offline channels for seamless customer experiences.

Dropshipping Models: Enable direct shipments from suppliers to customers, reducing handling times.

3.5 Sustainability Initiatives

Green Delivery Options: Using electric vehicles or optimizing delivery routes to reduce emissions.

Eco-Friendly Packaging: Encourages recycling and reduces waste in fulfillment operations.

Order fulfillment is a critical component of logistics, directly impacting customer satisfaction and business success. A well-structured order processing workflow ensures efficiency and accuracy, while proactive measures foster customer satisfaction through timely and error-free deliveries. The integration of technology further enhances order fulfillment by enabling automation, real-time tracking, and innovative solutions like AI and robotics. Businesses that excel in order fulfillment are better positioned to build customer loyalty, improve operational efficiency, and thrive in competitive markets.

Section 3: Advanced Topics in Logistics

Distribution Network Design

Designing an efficient distribution network is critical for the success of logistics and supply chain management. A well-planned network ensures the timely delivery of products, reduces operational costs, and enhances customer satisfaction. This chapter discusses the factors influencing network design, explores the trade-offs between centralized and decentralized networks, and examines tools for optimizing distribution networks.

1. Factors Influencing Network Design

Several factors affect the design of a distribution network, ranging from customer requirements to operational constraints. Understanding these factors is essential for creating a network that aligns with business goals.

1.1 Customer Requirements

Service Level Expectations: The network must support fast and reliable deliveries to meet customer demands.

Demand Patterns: Seasonal fluctuations and regional demand variations influence the placement of distribution centers.

1.2 Cost Considerations

Transportation Costs: Balancing inbound and outbound logistics costs is crucial for cost efficiency.

Warehousing Costs: The number and location of warehouses impact storage expenses.

1.3 Geographical Factors

Proximity to Markets: Distribution centers should be located close to major customer bases to reduce last-mile delivery costs.

Infrastructure Availability: The quality of transportation networks, such as roads, ports, and railways, affects the choice of locations.

1.4 Product Characteristics

Shelf Life: Products with shorter shelf lives, like perishable goods, require closer proximity to markets.

Handling Requirements: Specialized facilities may be needed for fragile or hazardous goods.

1.5 Supply Chain Strategies

Sourcing Decisions: The location of suppliers impacts transportation and inventory placement.

Production Strategies: Centralized production might require more robust distribution networks to cover large areas.

1.6 Regulatory and Environmental Factors

Taxation and Tariffs: Regional taxes, duties, and trade agreements influence network design.

Sustainability Goals: Companies increasingly consider eco-friendly network configurations to reduce carbon footprints.

2. Centralized vs. Decentralized Networks

The structure of a distribution network can be broadly classified as centralized or decentralized. Each approach has its advantages and trade-offs.

2.1 Centralized Networks

In a centralized network, distribution is managed from a single or few locations.

Advantages:

Cost Efficiency: Lower inventory and warehousing costs due to economies of scale.

Better Control: Centralized operations allow for easier standardization and coordination.

Reduced Complexity: Fewer locations simplify management and oversight.

Disadvantages:

Longer Delivery Times: Products may need to travel longer distances, impacting lead times.

Higher Transportation Costs: Increased outbound logistics expenses for distant markets.

Suitable For:

Businesses with predictable demand and high-volume, low-variation products.

2.2 Decentralized Networks

In a decentralized network, multiple distribution centers are spread across regions.

Advantages:

Faster Delivery: Closer proximity to customers reduces lead times and enhances service levels.

Lower Transportation Costs: Shorter delivery distances reduce last-mile costs.

Flexibility: Better adaptability to regional demand fluctuations.

Disadvantages:

Higher Inventory Costs: Maintaining stock at multiple locations increases holding costs.

Operational Complexity: Managing multiple facilities requires advanced coordination.

Suitable For:

Companies with diverse product lines and variable regional demand patterns.

2.3 Choosing the Right Approach

The decision between centralized and decentralized networks depends on factors such as market size, customer expectations, and product characteristics. A hybrid approach, combining elements of both models, is often employed to balance cost and service efficiency.

3. Tools for Optimizing Distribution Networks

Optimizing a distribution network involves using advanced tools and methodologies to ensure cost-effectiveness and service excellence.

3.1 Network Modeling and Simulation

What It Is: Modeling tools create virtual representations of distribution networks to test various configurations.

Applications: Identify bottlenecks, evaluate cost implications, and predict the impact of changes.

Example Tools: Llamasoft Supply Chain Guru, AnyLogic.

3.2 Geographic Information Systems (GIS)

What It Is: GIS tools analyze geographical data to determine optimal warehouse locations and transportation routes.

Benefits: Visualize proximity to markets, infrastructure, and population density.

Example Tools: ArcGIS, QGIS.

3.3 Optimization Algorithms

What They Are: Algorithms like linear programming and genetic algorithms help solve complex distribution problems.

Applications: Optimize inventory placement, transportation routes, and facility locations.

Benefits: Provide data-driven solutions for cost and time efficiency.

3.4 Big Data Analytics

What It Is: Analyzing large datasets to uncover trends and insights that influence network design.

Applications: Demand forecasting, customer segmentation, and route optimization.

Example Tools: Hadoop, Spark.

3.5 Advanced Transportation Management Systems (TMS)

What It Is: TMS software optimizes shipping routes, carrier selection, and freight costs.

Applications: Real-time tracking, load optimization, and performance analytics.

Example Tools: Oracle TMS, SAP TMS.

3.6 Artificial Intelligence and Machine Learning

What It Is: AI and machine learning tools predict demand, optimize inventory, and recommend network adjustments.

Applications: Dynamic inventory positioning and predictive maintenance.

Distribution network design is a complex but critical aspect of logistics management. By considering key factors such as customer needs, costs, and geographical constraints, businesses can choose between centralized and decentralized models—or adopt a hybrid approach. The use of advanced tools like GIS, optimization algorithms, and AI enhances decision-making and ensures that networks are agile, cost-efficient, and aligned with long-term business goals. An optimized distribution network not only reduces costs but also improves service levels, providing a competitive edge in today's dynamic market landscape.

Reverse Logistics

Reverse logistics, the process of moving goods from the point of consumption back to the point of origin for return, recycling, remanufacturing, or disposal, plays a critical role in the modern supply chain. It involves the handling of returned products, waste, defective goods, and product end-of-life issues, and is increasingly gaining importance as businesses recognize its impact on customer satisfaction, cost management, and sustainability.

This chapter delves into the importance of managing returns, explores the reverse supply chain processes, and discusses the cost and sustainability benefits of reverse logistics.

1. Importance of Managing Returns

The management of returns, often viewed as a secondary or afterthought function, is now being recognized as an essential component of overall logistics strategy. Efficient returns management directly affects customer satisfaction, company profitability, and brand reputation. In fact, the rise of e-commerce, along with consumer expectations for easy and hassle-free returns, has made returns management more important than ever.

1.1 Customer Satisfaction and Retention

Convenience for Customers: Offering a smooth and straightforward return process enhances the overall customer experience. Studies indicate that companies offering free returns or hassle-free return policies often see higher levels of customer satisfaction and loyalty.

Brand Image: An efficient return process reflects positively on the company's customer service capabilities. On the contrary, poor returns management can lead to frustration, negative reviews, and a loss of repeat business.

Competitive Advantage: In competitive industries, where similar products and services are offered, the quality of returns management can become a deciding factor for consumers. Companies that offer an easy, no-questions-asked returns policy attract more buyers, especially in e-commerce.

1.2 Cost Implications of Poor Returns Management

Increased Operational Costs: Inefficient returns processes lead to excess labor, storage, and transportation costs. Poor handling can result in the need for excessive returns processing or even product disposal when reprocessing is not an option.

Product Value Loss: Returned products that cannot be resold in the same condition, such as used or damaged items, often result in a loss of product value, reducing the profitability of the business.

Impact on Inventory: Returns can create discrepancies in inventory levels, making it difficult to maintain accurate stock counts, which affects inventory planning, forecasting, and replenishment strategies.

Effective management of returns not only reduces the associated costs but also ensures that the returned items are properly accounted for, repurposed, or reused, maximizing the value of the returned goods.

2. Reverse Supply Chain Processes

Reverse logistics involves a series of processes aimed at managing the flow of goods in the reverse direction—from customers back to businesses, manufacturers, or service centers for repair, refurbishment, recycling, or disposal. The complexity of these processes can vary depending on the nature of the goods being returned, the reasons for the return, and the business's ability to manage these returns effectively.

2.1 Product Return Initiation

Consumer Returns: The reverse logistics process begins when a consumer initiates a return, which can be for reasons such as product dissatisfaction, defects, or excess inventory. Consumers usually contact customer service or use online portals to start the return process.

Return Authorization: In most cases, businesses require a return authorization (RMA - Return Merchandise Authorization) to ensure the product meets the return criteria and that the return is legitimate.

2.2 Transportation and Movement of Goods

Shipping Back to Centralized Locations: The returned products are often shipped back to a designated return center, warehouse, or distribution hub for processing. For certain products, this may also involve transportation back to the manufacturer or retailer's central office.

Routing to Appropriate Facilities: Based on the product type, the returned goods may be directed to different locations for different purposes, such as restocking, refurbishing, recycling, or disposal.

2.3 Processing of Returns

Inspection and Sorting: Once the goods arrive at the returns facility, they are inspected for damage, wear, or defects. The inspection process determines whether the item is suitable for restocking, refurbishment, recycling, or disposal.

Repackaging or Refurbishing: Items that are in good condition can be restocked and sold as new or refurbished. In cases where products can be repaired or refurbished (such as electronics, appliances, or machinery), they are sent to repair or refurbishment centers.

Product Disposal: Some products may be damaged beyond repair or have reached the end of their usable life. These items are often sent for recycling or responsible disposal, adhering to environmental standards.

2.4 Restocking and Resale

Reselling Returned Goods: Products that are in new or refurbished condition can be resold at full price, or sometimes at a discounted rate. The decision to restock the item for resale depends on its condition and market demand.

Inventory Management: Businesses must have systems in place to accurately track returned products in the inventory system, ensuring that items are either returned to stock or marked as unsellable based on the inspection results.

2.5 Recycling and Disposal

Sustainability Initiatives: Many businesses are adopting reverse logistics processes that align with sustainability goals. Products that cannot be resold are often recycled to recover valuable raw materials, such as metals, plastics, and electronics components.

Compliance with Environmental Regulations: Reverse logistics ensures that businesses comply with environmental laws and regulations, particularly in industries that deal with hazardous materials or electronic waste.

3. Cost and Sustainability Benefits of Reverse Logistics

The reverse logistics process has the potential to create substantial cost savings and sustainability benefits, as companies seek to recover value from returned products and reduce waste.

3.1 Cost Savings

Recovering Value from Returns: By processing and reselling returned goods, companies can recover a portion of their investment, particularly for items that are still in good condition or can be refurbished. For instance, returned electronics can be repaired and resold, recovering much of the lost value.

Reduced Waste and Disposal Costs: Recycling returned goods and parts can significantly reduce the amount of waste sent to landfills. Companies may even recoup the value of the materials through resale or recycling programs.

Lowered Transportation Costs: Efficient reverse logistics can help reduce transportation costs associated with returns by consolidating shipments and optimizing routes for both forward and reverse flows.

Lower Inventory Costs: A well-managed reverse logistics process ensures returned products are processed quickly, allowing businesses to restock inventory promptly and reduce stockouts. Moreover, returns management can minimize the need for excess stock as businesses can rely on returns to replenish inventory.

3.2 Environmental and Sustainability Benefits

Reduction in Waste: Reverse logistics facilitates the recycling and reuse of products, preventing them from being discarded in landfills. This aligns with corporate sustainability goals and reduces the environmental footprint.

Resource Recovery: Valuable raw materials can be recovered from returned goods, especially in industries such as electronics. This reduces the need for new raw material extraction, helping conserve natural resources.

Extended Product Life Cycle: Reverse logistics enables the repair and refurbishment of products, thus extending the product's life cycle. For example, returned electronics can be refurbished and resold, reducing the need for new manufacturing and promoting the concept of a circular economy.

3.3 Customer Loyalty and Brand Reputation

Sustainability and Consumer Appeal: Consumers are increasingly concerned about the environmental impact of their purchases. Companies that incorporate reverse logistics processes, such as recycling or refurbishing, often enjoy higher customer loyalty due to their sustainability practices.

Transparency and Corporate Responsibility: Companies that emphasize their commitment to managing returns efficiently and sustainably can build strong, positive brand reputations. This creates trust among consumers who value environmental responsibility.

Reverse logistics is no longer just a reactive process—it's a strategic function that can drive cost savings, improve sustainability, and enhance customer satisfaction. Effective returns management is key to reducing operational costs, recovering value from returned goods, and contributing to environmental sustainability. By optimizing reverse logistics processes, businesses can not only improve their bottom line but also build stronger, more loyal customer relationships while contributing to the reduction of waste and promoting a more sustainable economy. As reverse logistics continues to evolve, businesses that invest in streamlined processes, cutting-edge technologies, and sustainability-driven practices will reap long-term benefits.

Cold Chain Logistics

Cold chain logistics refers to the process of managing the transportation, storage, and handling of temperature-sensitive products. These products require a controlled temperature environment throughout the supply chain to maintain their quality, safety, and efficacy. Cold chain logistics is crucial for industries such as pharmaceuticals, food and beverages, biotechnology, and chemicals, where temperature fluctuations can cause irreparable damage to products, leading to quality loss, health risks, and financial losses.

This chapter will explore an overview of cold chain management, challenges in temperature-controlled logistics, and best practices and innovations in the field of cold chain logistics.

1. Overview of Cold Chain Management

Cold chain management is the process of maintaining a consistent temperature environment for perishable goods, from the point of origin to the point of consumption. This process involves using specialized transportation (refrigerated trucks, containers, and ships), storage facilities (temperature-controlled warehouses), and advanced technologies to ensure that products remain within a specified temperature range throughout the journey.

1.1 Importance of Cold Chain Logistics

Perishable Goods Preservation: Products such as fresh food, pharmaceuticals (e.g., vaccines, insulin), and chemicals require specific temperature conditions to prevent degradation or contamination. Any break in the cold chain can render these products unsafe or unusable.

Health and Safety: For temperature-sensitive items like vaccines and blood products, maintaining the cold chain is a matter of public health and safety. Variations in temperature can compromise the potency of vaccines, potentially putting lives at risk.

Regulatory Compliance: Regulatory authorities, such as the U.S. Food and Drug Administration (FDA) and the European Medicines Agency (EMA), impose strict guidelines on the handling of temperature-sensitive products. Companies must ensure compliance with these regulations to avoid penalties, product recalls, and reputational damage.

1.2 Cold Chain Logistics in Key Industries

Pharmaceutical Industry: Vaccines, biologics, and certain medications need to be stored and transported within very specific temperature ranges, often from 2°C to 8°C (36°F to 46°F), or even in ultra-low temperature conditions (below -70°C) for some biological products.

Food Industry: Perishable foods, including meat, dairy, and frozen foods, must be kept at low temperatures to maintain freshness and prevent bacterial growth. The food industry often faces challenges with supply chain disruptions, such as power outages or delays, that can impact product quality.

Chemical Industry: Certain chemicals, such as specialty paints or adhesives, also require temperature control during transportation and storage to ensure they remain stable and effective.

2. Challenges in Temperature-Controlled Logistics

Cold chain logistics faces several challenges that can complicate the process of maintaining an optimal temperature range. These challenges require careful planning, monitoring, and the use of advanced technology.

2.1 Temperature Fluctuations

Equipment Failure: Refrigeration units in trucks, containers, and storage facilities may break down, leading to temperature fluctuations. If temperatures rise or fall outside the desired range, products may be compromised.

Manual Handling: Improper handling or incorrect loading/unloading processes can result in temperature fluctuations. For example, opening a refrigerated container during the unloading process can introduce warm air, causing temperature instability.

Seasonal Changes: Extreme weather conditions, such as hot summers or freezing winters, can exacerbate temperature control challenges. For example, refrigerated vehicles may struggle to maintain the correct temperature in extreme heat, while cold storage warehouses may require extra heating systems during winter months.

2.2 Monitoring and Visibility

Lack of Real-Time Data: Without continuous monitoring, it's difficult to detect temperature deviations in real-time. As a result, companies may not know that a product has been exposed to unacceptable conditions until it's too late.

Tracking and Transparency: Many companies still rely on traditional methods, such as paper logs, to monitor temperature conditions, which can be inaccurate and inefficient. Modern cold chain logistics demands a higher level of visibility and traceability throughout the supply chain.

Human Error: Temperature-sensitive products often pass through multiple stages and handlers. Any lapses in following the proper protocols—such as incorrect packing, mishandling during transit, or poor storage practices—can compromise the entire cold chain.

2.3 Regulatory Compliance

Global Standards: Compliance with local and international standards is a significant challenge, especially for companies that operate in multiple regions. Regulations governing the temperature limits, storage conditions, and documentation requirements vary across countries, requiring companies to adjust their processes accordingly.

Inspection and Documentation: Cold chain logistics also demands detailed documentation for compliance audits. Accurate record-keeping is crucial for regulatory inspections, yet many companies still face difficulties in maintaining the level of documentation required by authorities.

2.4 Infrastructure and Cost Constraints

High Operational Costs: Maintaining temperature-controlled environments is expensive, requiring significant investment in specialized equipment, such as refrigerated transport vehicles and cold storage facilities. These costs often translate into higher product prices, which can be a challenge for businesses operating on thin margins.

Limited Infrastructure in Developing Regions: While cold chain logistics infrastructure is well-established in developed markets, developing regions often lack the necessary infrastructure, including refrigerated transport, cold storage facilities, and trained personnel, to ensure the proper handling of temperature-sensitive goods.

Supply Chain Interruptions: Even a brief interruption in the cold chain, such as a delay at a port or a transportation issue, can lead to catastrophic losses, especially for perishable goods. This can be particularly problematic in global supply chains where products are transported across vast distances and multiple time zones.

3. Best Practices and Innovations in Cold Chain Logistics

To address the challenges in cold chain logistics and ensure the safe transportation of temperature-sensitive goods, companies are adopting best practices and innovative solutions that improve efficiency, reduce risk, and enhance compliance.

3.1 Real-Time Monitoring and Tracking

Internet of Things (IoT) Sensors: One of the most significant innovations in cold chain logistics is the use of IoT sensors that continuously monitor temperature, humidity, and other environmental conditions during transit. These sensors transmit real-time data to a central system, allowing companies to track conditions and receive alerts if temperature deviations occur.

Blockchain Technology: Blockchain is increasingly being used to enhance transparency and traceability in cold chain logistics. By creating a secure, tamper-proof ledger of product movements and environmental conditions, blockchain ensures that all parties in the supply chain can trust the data and documentation related to temperature-sensitive goods.

RFID and GPS Tracking: RFID tags and GPS systems are being integrated into cold chain processes to monitor and track products. These technologies enable real-time visibility of product locations and conditions, providing a higher level of control over the supply chain.

3.2 Advanced Packaging Solutions

Thermal Insulated Packaging: Advanced packaging materials, such as thermal blankets, phase change materials (PCMs), and insulated boxes, help maintain the desired temperature range for products during transportation. These packaging materials are designed to retain or absorb heat for long periods, protecting the product from temperature fluctuations.

Active vs. Passive Systems: Cold chain logistics often uses passive systems (such as insulated boxes) and active systems (such as refrigerated containers). Active systems are powered, keeping the product within a controlled temperature range throughout the journey, while passive systems rely on the insulation to maintain temperature.

3.3 Automation and Robotics

Automated Warehouses: Automation is increasingly being used in cold storage facilities to handle products efficiently while maintaining the required temperature conditions. Automated storage and retrieval systems (ASRS) can improve storage density, reduce human errors, and increase speed in handling temperature-sensitive products.

Robotic Handling: Robotics is used for sorting, packing, and transporting goods in temperature-controlled environments, reducing the need for manual labor and improving overall efficiency.

3.4 Sustainability Initiatives

Eco-Friendly Refrigerants: The refrigeration systems used in cold chain logistics often rely on hydrofluorocarbon (HFC) refrigerants, which contribute to global warming. The cold chain industry is now transitioning to more environmentally friendly refrigerants, such as hydrofluoroolefins (HFOs) or natural refrigerants, to reduce its carbon footprint.

Energy Efficiency: Energy-efficient technologies, such as solar-powered refrigeration systems or energy-efficient cold storage facilities, are being increasingly adopted to reduce energy consumption and operating costs in cold chain logistics.

3.5 Training and Compliance

Employee Training: Properly training personnel in cold chain management is essential. Employees must be educated on the handling of temperature-sensitive goods, safe storage procedures, and emergency response actions in the event of a temperature excursion.

Compliance Software: Companies are using compliance management software to ensure they meet regulatory requirements and track temperature records for inspections and audits. These software systems also provide alerts for any deviations from the required temperature ranges, ensuring prompt corrective actions.

Cold chain logistics plays a vital role in industries dealing with perishable, temperature-sensitive goods. Managing temperature fluctuations, ensuring real-time visibility, maintaining compliance with global regulations, and improving operational efficiencies are essential to ensuring product quality and safety. As demand for cold chain logistics grows, especially in pharmaceuticals and food products, businesses must embrace innovation, automation, and sustainable practices to address challenges and stay competitive in an increasingly complex supply chain landscape.

Third-Party Logistics (3PL) and Fourth-Party Logistics (4PL)

In the modern logistics landscape, businesses are increasingly turning to outsourcing to streamline their operations, enhance efficiency, and focus on core competencies. The terms Third-Party Logistics (3PL) and Fourth-Party Logistics (4PL) have gained prominence as organizations seek to leverage external expertise to manage their logistics functions. Understanding what 3PL and 4PL entail, along with the associated benefits, risks, and best practices in selecting the right logistics partner, is critical for optimizing the supply chain.

This chapter will provide an in-depth look at Third-Party Logistics (3PL) and Fourth-Party Logistics (4PL), discussing their differences, advantages and challenges, and key considerations when outsourcing logistics functions.

1. What Are 3PL and 4PL?

1.1 Third-Party Logistics (3PL)

Third-Party Logistics (3PL) refers to the outsourcing of logistics functions to an external provider. A 3PL provider is responsible for managing all or part of a company's supply chain activities, such as transportation, warehousing, inventory management, order fulfillment, and distribution. These providers typically operate independently from the company's core business and offer specialized logistics services to help optimize and streamline the supply chain.

Key Services Provided by 3PL:

Transportation Management: 3PL providers manage the movement of goods across various modes of transportation, including trucks, ships, planes, and rail.

Warehousing and Distribution: 3PL providers offer storage space and distribution services, often using advanced warehouse management systems (WMS) to track inventory and optimize order picking.

Inventory Management: 3PL providers may handle inventory control, replenishment, and stock management, allowing businesses to focus on other aspects of their operations.

Order Fulfillment: 3PLs manage the process of picking, packing, and shipping products to customers, ensuring that orders are fulfilled efficiently and accurately.

1.2 Fourth-Party Logistics (4PL)

Fourth-Party Logistics (4PL), also known as Lead Logistics Providers (LLP), goes a step further than 3PL by acting as an intermediary between the client and various 3PL providers. A 4PL is responsible for overseeing the entire logistics function for a business, managing the relationships with multiple 3PL providers, and integrating logistics operations into a seamless, end-to-end supply chain solution. Essentially, a 4PL provides a higher level of strategic oversight and coordination, offering a single point of contact for all logistics activities.

Key Functions of 4PL:

Supply Chain Management and Integration: 4PLs manage the entire supply chain from end to end, coordinating all aspects of logistics and ensuring that each part of the supply chain is working in harmony.

Third-Party Vendor Management: A 4PL oversees relationships with multiple 3PL providers and other external vendors, ensuring that the right partners are selected and the services are optimized.

Data Analytics and Reporting: 4PLs typically provide advanced analytics and reporting to help businesses monitor logistics performance, identify inefficiencies, and improve decision-making.

Technology Integration: A 4PL integrates various logistics technologies, such as Warehouse Management Systems (WMS) and Transportation Management Systems (TMS), into the client's supply chain for improved visibility, tracking, and performance.

Key Differences Between 3PL and 4PL:

Scope of Services: 3PL focuses on specific logistics functions (e.g., transportation, warehousing), while 4PL manages the entire supply chain and acts as the strategic partner that coordinates multiple 3PL providers.

Level of Involvement: 3PL providers handle day-to-day logistics tasks, whereas 4PL providers focus on high-level coordination, optimization, and strategic decision-making.

Ownership of Logistics Assets: 3PL providers may own and operate the logistics assets (e.g., warehouses, trucks), while 4PL providers typically do not own logistics assets but instead manage the network of service providers.

2. Benefits and Risks of Outsourcing Logistics

2.1 Benefits of Outsourcing Logistics to 3PL and 4PL Providers

Outsourcing logistics functions to a 3PL or 4PL provider can provide numerous benefits to a business. Some of the key advantages include:

2.1.1 Cost Savings

Lower Capital Investment: Outsourcing logistics allows businesses to avoid significant upfront investments in infrastructure, such as warehouses, trucks, and inventory management systems.

Economies of Scale: 3PLs and 4PLs often have access to a larger network of resources, enabling them to achieve economies of scale that individual businesses cannot match. This allows for more cost-effective transportation and storage solutions.

Reduced Operational Costs: By outsourcing logistics, companies can lower labor costs, reduce overheads associated with running a logistics department, and avoid expenses related to maintaining logistics infrastructure.

2.1.2 Expertise and Specialization

Access to Expertise: 3PLs and 4PLs specialize in logistics and supply chain management, bringing in-depth knowledge, industry best practices, and advanced technologies to optimize operations.

Technology Integration: Outsourcing logistics allows companies to benefit from the latest technology without having to invest in building or maintaining these systems in-house, such as advanced tracking, warehouse management, and data analytics tools.

Focus on Core Competencies: By outsourcing logistics, businesses can focus on their core competencies, such as product development, marketing, and sales, while leaving the complex logistics functions to experts.

2.1.3 Improved Service Levels

Faster Delivery: 3PLs and 4PLs leverage their networks and experience to optimize shipping routes and reduce lead times, leading to faster delivery times and improved customer satisfaction.

Scalability: Logistics partners can quickly scale up or down based on the company's needs. During peak seasons, businesses can easily access additional resources, such as extra storage or transportation capacity, without worrying about overcapacity or underutilization.

Global Reach: 3PLs and 4PLs often have international networks, enabling businesses to expand into new markets and manage global logistics without the complexities of setting up operations in multiple regions.

2.1.4 Risk Mitigation

Compliance and Regulations: Logistics providers stay up to date with the latest industry regulations and standards, helping businesses stay compliant with local and international laws and avoiding penalties.

Risk Diversification: By outsourcing logistics, companies can reduce the risks associated with owning and operating their logistics infrastructure, such as supply chain disruptions, equipment failures, and labor issues.

2.2 Risks of Outsourcing Logistics

Despite the many benefits, outsourcing logistics also comes with certain risks that companies should carefully consider:

2.2.1 Loss of Control

Limited Oversight: By outsourcing logistics, companies may lose direct control over the day-to-day operations, which could lead to challenges in managing service quality and ensuring that the logistics partner is fully aligned with the company's goals.

Quality Concerns: If a 3PL or 4PL provider does not maintain the same quality standards as the company, it can lead to operational inefficiencies, errors in order fulfillment, and dissatisfied customers.

2.2.2 Dependence on the Logistics Partner

Single Point of Failure: Relying on a single logistics partner for critical supply chain functions can create a potential vulnerability. Any issues with the provider, such as financial instability, operational disruptions, or labor strikes, can severely impact the business.

Reduced Flexibility: Relying on an external logistics provider may limit the company's ability to respond quickly to changing market conditions, customer demands, or unforeseen events in the supply chain.

2.2.3 Security and Confidentiality Risks

Data Security: Outsourcing logistics may involve sharing sensitive data, such as customer information, inventory levels, and pricing strategies, with third-party providers. If not handled securely, this data could be at risk of breaches, cyberattacks, or misuse.

Intellectual Property Risks: Companies must ensure that logistics partners take adequate measures to protect intellectual property, such as product designs or proprietary technologies, from theft or unauthorized sharing.

2.2.4 Hidden Costs

Unexpected Expenses: While outsourcing logistics can reduce certain operational costs, there may be hidden fees or unexpected costs, such as service charges for additional handling, storage, or expedited shipping that were not anticipated in the initial contract.

Inflexible Contract Terms: Some 3PL or 4PL contracts may lock companies into long-term agreements with rigid terms, making it difficult to adjust services or pricing if the business's needs change.

3. Choosing the Right Logistics Partner

Selecting the right logistics partner is a critical decision that can significantly impact the efficiency, cost-effectiveness, and success of a business's supply chain operations. When choosing a 3PL or 4PL provider, businesses should consider the following factors:

3.1 Expertise and Reputation

Industry Knowledge: Ensure the logistics partner has experience in your specific industry, whether it's e-commerce, healthcare, or manufacturing. Specialized knowledge can ensure that your products are handled efficiently and in compliance with regulations.

Reputation: Research the provider's track record and reputation in the market. Look for customer reviews, case studies, and testimonials that demonstrate their ability to deliver high-quality services.

3.2 Service Capabilities

Range of Services: Determine whether the provider offers the specific services you need, such as transportation management, warehousing, or inventory control. The more comprehensive their offerings, the better they can manage all aspects of your logistics.

Scalability: Ensure that the logistics partner can handle fluctuations in demand and scale services up or down as needed.

3.3 Technology and Innovation

Technology Integration: Choose a logistics partner that uses advanced technology, such as real-time tracking, warehouse automation, and data analytics, to optimize the supply chain and improve visibility.

Innovation: A good logistics partner will stay ahead of industry trends and continuously innovate to improve efficiency and reduce costs.

3.4 Communication and Transparency

Clear Communication: The logistics provider should offer transparent communication and provide clear reporting on key metrics, such as order status, inventory levels, and delivery times.

Customer Support: Ensure the logistics partner offers reliable customer service to address issues promptly and ensure smooth operations.

3.5 Cost and Contract Terms

Cost-Effectiveness: While cost is an important factor, it should not be the sole consideration. Evaluate the overall value offered by the logistics partner, considering both direct and indirect costs.

Flexible Terms: Look for a logistics partner that offers flexible contract terms, allowing you to adjust services and pricing if necessary.

Outsourcing logistics to a 3PL or 4PL provider can significantly improve supply chain efficiency, reduce costs, and enhance customer satisfaction. However, businesses must carefully weigh the benefits and risks of outsourcing logistics and choose the right partner based on expertise, capabilities, technology, and alignment with business goals. By selecting the right logistics partner and managing the relationship effectively, companies can create a more agile and responsive supply chain that supports growth and success.

Last-Mile Delivery

The final leg of the logistics journey, known as last-mile delivery, is one of the most critical and complex components of the supply chain. It involves the movement of goods from a transportation hub or distribution center to the final destination, typically the customer's door. The efficiency and effectiveness of last-mile delivery play a major role in customer satisfaction, cost management, and overall supply chain performance.

This chapter will explore the challenges associated with last-mile logistics, the role of technology in optimizing last-mile delivery, and some of the innovations, such as drones and autonomous vehicles, that are shaping the future of this vital logistics function.

1. Challenges in Last-Mile Logistics

The challenges in last-mile logistics are numerous and can vary significantly depending on the nature of the goods being delivered, the geographical area, and the customer base. The following are some of the most common challenges faced in last-mile delivery:

1.1 High Costs

Last-mile delivery often represents the most expensive part of the logistics chain, accounting for up to 50% of total delivery costs. This high cost can be attributed to factors such as:

Labor-intensive processes: Delivery drivers must navigate complex routes, and in densely populated urban areas, drivers may make numerous stops, leading to inefficiency.

Small order sizes: With the rise of e-commerce, especially in industries like fashion and electronics, customers frequently place small orders, which increase the number of deliveries and overall transportation costs.

Delivery delays: Unexpected issues such as traffic congestion, road closures, and incorrect address information can delay deliveries and add to costs.

1.2 Traffic and Urban Congestion

Urban areas, especially densely populated cities, present significant challenges for last-mile delivery. Traffic congestion can lead to delays, longer delivery windows, and increased fuel consumption, all of which add to operational costs. Finding efficient routes through crowded urban environments while adhering to strict time windows is a major logistical challenge.

1.3 Delivery Accuracy and Customer Expectations

Customer expectations have been rising steadily, driven by the growth of e-commerce giants like Amazon. Customers demand faster delivery times, precise tracking, and reliable service. If a package is delayed, misplaced, or delivered incorrectly, it can significantly harm customer satisfaction and brand reputation.

1.4 Environmental Impact

Last-mile delivery's environmental impact has become a growing concern, especially as e-commerce and demand for faster deliveries continue to rise. The increasing number of delivery vehicles on the road contributes to air pollution, traffic congestion, and carbon emissions. This raises concerns among businesses, governments, and consumers about the sustainability of delivery practices.

1.5 Last-Mile Delivery in Rural Areas

While urban areas may struggle with congestion, rural areas face their own set of challenges in last-mile delivery. Longer distances, fewer transportation options, and lower delivery volumes make rural deliveries more expensive and less efficient. Companies may also have trouble finding reliable delivery partners or personnel in remote regions.

2. Role of Technology in Last-Mile Delivery

Technology has become a key enabler in addressing the challenges associated with last-mile delivery. By integrating advanced systems, companies can optimize routes, improve tracking accuracy, and increase customer satisfaction. Some of the primary ways technology is improving last-mile delivery include:

2.1 Route Optimization Software

Advanced route optimization software uses real-time traffic data, historical delivery patterns, and algorithms to determine the most efficient routes for delivery drivers. These systems take into account variables like road conditions, weather, and traffic to ensure that goods are delivered as quickly and cost-effectively as possible. Route optimization helps reduce fuel consumption, improve delivery times, and cut down on costs associated with inefficient driving.

2.2 Real-Time Tracking

Real-time tracking technology allows customers to track their orders throughout the delivery process, from the warehouse to their doorstep. Not only does this increase customer satisfaction by providing transparency, but it also helps delivery teams monitor the status of shipments in real time. In case of delays or unexpected issues, companies can notify customers proactively, managing expectations and improving the overall customer experience.

2.3 Predictive Analytics

Predictive analytics uses historical data and machine learning models to predict delivery outcomes and potential disruptions before they occur. This allows logistics companies to forecast demand, adjust routes dynamically, and provide more accurate delivery time windows. For instance, predictive analytics can anticipate traffic bottlenecks or weather-related delays, helping businesses plan alternate routes or adjust staffing levels as needed.

2.4 Autonomous Delivery Vehicles

The advent of autonomous delivery vehicles is transforming last-mile logistics. These vehicles, including drones, self-driving cars, and robotic delivery devices, can potentially reduce the reliance on human drivers and lower delivery costs. Autonomous vehicles can operate 24/7, avoid human error, and provide faster delivery speeds, all while reducing fuel consumption and environmental impact.

2.5 Delivery Drones

Drones are one of the most exciting technologies in last-mile delivery. These unmanned aerial vehicles can deliver small parcels over short distances, particularly in hard-to-reach or congested urban areas. Drones offer significant advantages, such as:

Speed: Drones can fly directly from the warehouse to the destination, bypassing traffic and reducing delivery time significantly.

Cost savings: Once implemented on a large scale, drones can help reduce labor and transportation costs, making deliveries more affordable.

Environmental benefits: Since drones are electric-powered, they produce fewer emissions than traditional delivery vehicles, contributing to a more sustainable logistics network.

However, drones also face regulatory challenges, such as air traffic control restrictions, safety concerns, and limited payload capacities, which can hinder their widespread adoption.

3. Innovations Like Drones and Autonomous Vehicles

The future of last-mile delivery is heavily influenced by innovations in drones and autonomous vehicles. These technologies are not just futuristic concepts but are already being tested and deployed by companies in various parts of the world. Their adoption could drastically change the way goods are delivered, particularly in urban settings.

3.1 Drones in Last-Mile Delivery

As previously mentioned, drones have the potential to revolutionize last-mile logistics. Companies like Amazon,

Google, and UPS have already been testing drone delivery services, with trials taking place in cities and rural areas alike. Key advantages of drone delivery include:

Reduced delivery times: Drones can deliver packages in minutes instead of hours, helping businesses meet the growing demand for faster delivery services.

Cost efficiency: Drones, in the long run, can lower the overall cost of last-mile delivery by reducing the need for human drivers and traditional delivery vehicles.

Access to remote locations: Drones are particularly useful in rural areas or locations where traditional delivery trucks might struggle to reach.

However, there are still several obstacles to widespread adoption, such as regulatory approval, airspace congestion, privacy concerns, and limited battery life. Despite these challenges, many logistics companies continue to invest heavily in drone technology, with the expectation that they will become an integral part of the logistics landscape in the coming years.

3.2 Autonomous Vehicles in Last-Mile Delivery

Another promising innovation is the development of autonomous vehicles for last-mile delivery. Companies like Nuro and Starship Technologies have developed self-driving delivery vehicles and robots that are already being tested in cities for local deliveries. These vehicles are equipped with advanced sensors, GPS systems, and machine learning algorithms that enable them to navigate roads and deliver packages without human intervention.

Some benefits of autonomous vehicles in last-mile delivery include:

Cost savings: By eliminating the need for human drivers, autonomous vehicles can significantly reduce labor costs, making deliveries more affordable for businesses.

24/7 availability: Autonomous vehicles do not require rest periods and can operate around the clock, potentially reducing delivery times and increasing delivery capacity.

Sustainability: Many autonomous delivery vehicles are electric, contributing to a reduction in emissions and helping companies meet their sustainability goals.

However, autonomous vehicles still face challenges, including regulatory approval, safety concerns, and technological limitations. As with drones, these vehicles must adhere to strict safety regulations and ensure they can handle complex urban environments.

Last-mile delivery is an essential, yet challenging, component of the logistics process. With rising customer expectations, increased demand for faster deliveries, and growing environmental concerns, the pressure on businesses to innovate in last-mile logistics has never been greater. Technology is playing a crucial role in overcoming these challenges, with solutions like route optimization software, real-time tracking, and predictive analytics enabling companies to deliver more efficiently.

Moreover, innovations like drones and autonomous vehicles have the potential to reshape the future of last-mile delivery. While regulatory and technological hurdles remain, the ongoing investment in these innovations suggests that they will play a key role in the evolution of the logistics industry.

As businesses continue to adapt to the changing landscape, staying on top of the latest technological advancements and embracing new solutions will be crucial for maintaining a competitive edge in the rapidly evolving world of last-mile delivery.

Section 4: Technology and Innovation in Logistics

Digital Transformation in Logistics

The logistics industry is undergoing a significant digital transformation, driven by advancements in Internet of Things (IoT), Artificial Intelligence (AI), and Big Data technologies. These innovations are helping businesses streamline their operations, reduce costs, improve customer satisfaction, and enhance supply chain visibility. As the demand for faster, more efficient logistics services continues to rise, digital technologies are proving to be critical in transforming the way goods are managed and delivered.

This chapter will explore the role of IoT, AI, and big data in logistics, the use of real-time tracking and monitoring systems, and the benefits of digital logistics solutions.

1. Role of IoT, AI, and Big Data in Logistics

1.1 Internet of Things (IoT)

The Internet of Things (IoT) refers to the network of physical devices embedded with sensors, software, and other technologies that enable them to connect and exchange data over the internet. In logistics, IoT is revolutionizing operations by providing real-time visibility and control over goods in transit, warehouses, and distribution centers.

Key applications of IoT in logistics include:

Asset Tracking: IoT-enabled sensors allow logistics companies to track the location and condition of goods throughout the supply chain. For instance, RFID tags and GPS sensors can be used to monitor the movement of inventory and vehicles, providing real-time updates on their location.

Fleet Management: By equipping trucks, vans, and other vehicles with IoT devices, logistics companies can monitor the performance of their fleets, such as vehicle speed, fuel consumption, and maintenance needs. This helps in optimizing routes, reducing downtime, and ensuring vehicle safety.

Condition Monitoring: For sensitive or perishable goods, IoT sensors can monitor temperature, humidity, and other environmental factors to ensure that products are stored and transported under optimal conditions, reducing the risk of spoilage or damage.

Warehouse Automation: IoT devices in warehouses can track inventory levels, monitor warehouse equipment, and improve stock accuracy. These devices can communicate directly with the warehouse management system (WMS) to trigger reordering when stock levels fall below a certain threshold.

1.2 Artificial Intelligence (AI)

Artificial Intelligence (AI) is a transformative technology in logistics, enabling machines to simulate human intelligence. AI-powered solutions are being applied in various areas of logistics, from route optimization and predictive maintenance to demand forecasting and customer service.

Key applications of AI in logistics include:

Predictive Analytics: AI algorithms analyze historical data, market trends, and external factors (such as weather or traffic) to predict future demand and optimize supply chain planning. By forecasting demand more accurately, businesses can adjust inventory levels, manage lead times, and avoid stockouts or overstocking.

Route Optimization: AI algorithms can analyze real-time traffic data, road conditions, and other variables to determine the most efficient delivery routes. This not only reduces delivery times but also helps in minimizing fuel consumption and lowering transportation costs.

Automation of Routine Tasks: AI can automate routine logistics tasks, such as order processing, inventory management, and documentation. For example, robotic process automation (RPA) can be used to streamline tasks like updating inventory records, freeing up human resources for more strategic activities.

Chatbots and Customer Support: AI-powered chatbots are increasingly being used to enhance customer service. These chatbots can respond to customer inquiries about delivery status, order tracking, and shipping updates, providing faster and more efficient customer support.

1.3 Big Data

Big Data refers to the vast amounts of structured and unstructured data generated by businesses every day. In logistics, big data analytics involves the collection, processing, and analysis of data from various sources, such as sensors, transaction records, and customer interactions, to derive actionable insights.

Key applications of big data in logistics include:

Supply Chain Optimization: Big data allows logistics companies to analyze patterns and trends across the supply chain, such as lead times, transportation routes, and supplier performance. By identifying inefficiencies and bottlenecks, companies can make data-driven decisions to optimize their supply chain processes.

Demand Forecasting: Big data analytics can improve demand forecasting by analyzing historical sales data, customer preferences, and external factors (such as market conditions or seasonality). Accurate demand forecasting helps businesses plan inventory levels, manage production schedules, and reduce costs associated with excess inventory or stockouts.

Risk Management: Big data enables companies to identify potential risks and disruptions in the supply chain. By analyzing data from multiple sources, such as weather reports, geopolitical events, and supplier performance, logistics companies can anticipate risks and develop mitigation strategies.

Customer Insights: By analyzing customer data, businesses can gain insights into customer behavior, preferences, and delivery expectations. These insights can be used to improve the customer experience, tailor marketing strategies, and optimize delivery options.

2. Real-Time Tracking and Monitoring Systems

The demand for real-time visibility into the status of goods, vehicles, and inventory is one of the driving forces behind digital transformation in logistics. Real-time tracking and monitoring systems provide stakeholders with up-to-date information on the location, condition, and status of shipments.

2.1 Benefits of Real-Time Tracking

Improved Visibility: Real-time tracking provides end-to-end visibility into the movement of goods, helping businesses and customers stay informed about delivery status. Customers can track their orders from the warehouse to the final destination, ensuring transparency and enhancing trust.

Reduced Delays and Bottlenecks: By monitoring the movement of goods in real time, logistics companies can identify potential delays or bottlenecks in the supply chain and take corrective actions to mitigate these issues. For instance, if a delivery vehicle is stuck in traffic, a company can reroute it to avoid delays.

Enhanced Customer Experience: Real-time tracking allows businesses to provide accurate delivery windows and updates to customers, improving satisfaction. Automated notifications about shipment status or potential delays can keep customers informed and reduce anxiety.

Inventory Management: Real-time monitoring systems help track inventory levels in warehouses, ensuring that stock is available when needed and minimizing the risk of stockouts or overstocking. This improves inventory turnover and enhances supply chain efficiency.

2.2 Applications of Real-Time Tracking in Logistics

Fleet Management: Real-time tracking systems monitor the location, speed, and performance of delivery vehicles. Fleet managers can use this information to optimize routes, reduce idle time, and ensure that vehicles are operating efficiently.

Temperature-Controlled Goods: For perishable items, real-time monitoring of environmental factors such as temperature and humidity ensures that goods are transported under optimal conditions. Alerts can be set up to notify logistics managers if a shipment is at risk of deviating from required conditions.

Supply Chain Visibility Platforms: Many logistics companies now use cloud-based platforms that integrate real-time tracking and monitoring data from various sources, such as GPS devices, sensors, and weather reports. These platforms provide a centralized view of the entire supply chain, enabling better decision-making and collaboration among stakeholders.

3. Benefits of Digital Logistics

The integration of IoT, AI, big data, and real-time tracking technologies into logistics operations brings a host of benefits for businesses, customers, and the environment. The key benefits of digital logistics include:

3.1 Increased Efficiency

By leveraging real-time data and advanced analytics, logistics companies can streamline their operations and make more informed decisions. Automated processes, predictive maintenance, and optimized routes reduce operational inefficiencies, saving time and money.

3.2 Enhanced Customer Satisfaction

Digital logistics technologies help businesses meet customer demands for faster, more reliable delivery. Real-time tracking, accurate delivery windows, and proactive communication about potential delays contribute to a better customer experience and higher satisfaction.

3.3 Cost Reduction

Digital transformation allows logistics companies to reduce costs by optimizing routes, improving inventory management, and automating routine tasks. By lowering transportation costs, improving asset utilization, and reducing waste, businesses can achieve significant savings.

3.4 Better Decision-Making

The integration of big data and AI enables data-driven decision-making, which leads to better forecasting, risk management, and supply chain planning. With access to real-time data and predictive analytics, businesses can respond more quickly to market fluctuations and customer demands.

3.5 Sustainability

Digital logistics solutions, particularly those powered by AI and IoT, help optimize transportation routes, reduce fuel consumption, and lower carbon emissions. Additionally, better inventory management and real-time monitoring can reduce waste and promote sustainability in logistics operations.

The digital transformation of logistics is reshaping the industry by improving efficiency, enhancing customer satisfaction, and driving cost savings. The integration of IoT, AI, and big data allows businesses to gain real-time visibility, optimize operations, and make better decisions. As technology continues to evolve, digital logistics will play an even more critical role in meeting the demands of the modern supply chain, ensuring that companies remain competitive, agile, and sustainable in an increasingly complex logistics landscape.

Warehouse Automation and Robotics

Warehouse automation and robotics are revolutionizing the logistics industry by enhancing efficiency, reducing labor costs, improving accuracy, and enabling faster throughput in warehouse operations. The integration of automated storage and retrieval systems (AS/RS) and robotics is not just a trend but a significant shift that is shaping the future of warehousing. This chapter will delve into the key components of warehouse automation, the benefits and challenges associated with automation, and the future trends in warehouse robotics.

1. Automated Storage and Retrieval Systems (AS/RS)

Automated Storage and Retrieval Systems (AS/RS) are one of the most widely used forms of warehouse automation. These systems utilize machines to automatically store and retrieve goods from specific locations within a warehouse, minimizing the need for manual intervention. AS/RS are designed to increase storage density, optimize warehouse space, and reduce human error.

1.1 Components of AS/RS

Storage Racks: These are structured shelving systems that store goods. The racks are usually designed in a way that allows for maximum storage capacity while maintaining easy accessibility for retrieval.

Automated Retrieval Machines (ARM): These machines retrieve products from storage racks. They move along predefined tracks and can be controlled via centralized systems to pick the right item from a specific location.

Conveyor Systems: These systems move items between the storage and retrieval machines and the picking or shipping areas, helping to streamline the flow of materials within the warehouse.

Warehouse Control Systems (WCS): This is the software layer that manages the operation of the AS/RS, ensuring that machines and conveyors work together efficiently. The WCS integrates with other systems such as warehouse management systems (WMS) for seamless coordination.

1.2 How AS/RS Work

AS/RS systems work by automatically placing inventory into storage locations, which are organized based on factors like size, weight, and demand frequency. When an order is placed, the system retrieves the required items by sending an automated retrieval machine to the correct location. This minimizes human labor and reduces errors in item retrieval.

AS/RS can be designed for a variety of applications, including high-bay storage (storing items at high heights), unit-load AS/RS (handling large, heavy items), and mini-load AS/RS (handling smaller items or totes).

2. Benefits and Challenges of Warehouse Automation

2.1 Benefits of Warehouse Automation

Increased Efficiency and Speed: One of the primary benefits of warehouse automation is the increase in operational efficiency. Automated systems can perform tasks such as storing, retrieving, and sorting goods much faster than human workers, which leads to faster order fulfillment. For instance, AS/RS can operate 24/7 without the need for breaks, leading to more throughput.

Improved Accuracy and Reduced Errors: Automation reduces the chances of human error in tasks such as picking, sorting, and inventory management. This leads to more accurate order fulfillment, reducing the risk of costly mistakes and improving customer satisfaction.

Space Optimization: Automation allows for better use of warehouse space by enabling denser storage arrangements, such as vertical storage. This is particularly beneficial in areas where real estate costs are high or storage space is limited.

Cost Reduction: While the upfront cost of implementing automation can be significant, the long-term benefits include reduced labor costs, improved productivity, and lower operating expenses. Automation minimizes the need for manual labor, cutting down on staffing requirements and associated costs like overtime pay and insurance.

Improved Safety: Automation can reduce workplace injuries by taking over dangerous or physically demanding tasks. Machines, such as robotic arms, can handle heavy lifting and repetitive movements that would otherwise pose a risk to human workers.

2.2 Challenges of Warehouse Automation

High Initial Investment: The initial cost of implementing warehouse automation systems, including AS/RS, robotics, and the necessary software infrastructure, can be very high. This can be a barrier for smaller businesses or companies with limited capital.

Integration with Existing Systems: Warehouse automation systems need to be seamlessly integrated with existing systems such as warehouse management systems (WMS) and enterprise resource planning (ERP) systems. This integration can be complex and time-consuming.

Maintenance Costs: Automated systems require regular maintenance and occasional repairs to ensure optimal performance. The maintenance costs associated with automation systems can be significant, particularly if the systems are complex or specialized.

Technical Skill Requirements: The workforce must have the necessary technical skills to operate and maintain automated systems. There is a growing need for skilled workers in fields such as robotics, software development, and system integration, which can present challenges for companies in finding the right talent.

Flexibility Limitations: Automation systems can be highly efficient for standardized operations, but they may be less adaptable to changes in the types of goods being stored or retrieved. This can limit flexibility if the business needs to handle a wide range of products or adjust to sudden changes in demand.

3. Future Trends in Warehouse Robotics

The future of warehouse robotics is promising, with continuous innovations in automation technology. Robotics and automation are becoming more intelligent, flexible, and collaborative, offering new solutions to meet the demands of fast-paced e-commerce and global supply chains. Some of the key trends shaping the future of warehouse robotics include:

3.1 Collaborative Robots (Cobots)

Collaborative robots, or cobots, are designed to work alongside human workers in a shared workspace. Unlike traditional robots that operate in isolation, cobots can work safely and efficiently alongside humans, handling repetitive tasks while humans focus on more complex or value-added activities. Cobots can be used in picking, sorting, and packing operations, enhancing productivity and reducing strain on human workers.

The key advantage of cobots is their flexibility. They can be easily reprogrammed to handle different tasks, making them ideal for dynamic warehouse environments. Cobots also typically require less infrastructure and can be deployed faster than traditional robotic systems.

3.2 Artificial Intelligence and Machine Learning

AI and machine learning are being integrated into warehouse robotics to enable smarter decision-making and enhanced performance. With the help of AI algorithms, robots can analyze vast amounts of data to improve their tasks over time. For instance, robots can optimize their picking routes by learning from past operations and adjusting their movements to improve efficiency.

Machine learning also helps robots adapt to changing environments. As a warehouse's layout changes or product sizes vary, robots powered by machine learning can autonomously adjust their behavior to continue performing tasks with minimal human intervention.

3.3 Autonomous Mobile Robots (AMRs)

Autonomous mobile robots (AMRs) are becoming increasingly popular in warehouses. Unlike traditional Automated Guided

Vehicles (AGVs), which rely on predefined tracks, AMRs navigate dynamically using onboard sensors and cameras, allowing them to adapt to changes in the environment. AMRs are used for tasks such as transporting goods, replenishing stock, and assisting with order fulfillment.

AMRs can work in collaboration with humans, driving efficiency and safety by automating material handling and reducing the need for human workers to perform tasks like lifting and transporting heavy loads. They can also be programmed to optimize their routes, increasing throughput and reducing the time spent moving materials from one place to another.

3.4 Drone Technology

Drones are being explored as an innovative solution for inventory management and stocktaking in warehouses. Equipped with cameras, RFID scanners, and other sensors, drones can quickly scan barcodes and perform stock counts in hard-to-reach areas. This drastically reduces the time and labor required for manual stocktaking.

In the future, drones may also play a role in last-mile delivery, particularly in urban environments where they can bypass road traffic and provide faster delivery times. Drone technology is still in the early stages of implementation in logistics, but it holds great promise for enhancing warehouse operations.

3.5 Internet of Things (IoT) and Robotics Integration

The integration of IoT with warehouse robotics is another emerging trend. IoT sensors enable robots to communicate with other devices in the warehouse, such as conveyor belts, automated storage systems, and other robots. This network of connected devices allows for more efficient coordination and real-time decision-making.

For example, if a robot detects a delay in its path due to an obstacle or congestion, it can communicate with other robots or the warehouse management system to reroute or adjust its operations. The integration of IoT with robotics also allows for predictive maintenance, where robots can detect potential failures before they happen, minimizing downtime.

Warehouse automation and robotics are revolutionizing the logistics and supply chain industry, providing significant benefits in terms of efficiency, accuracy, and cost reduction. Automated storage and retrieval systems (AS/RS) have already demonstrated their ability to streamline operations, and as technology continues to evolve, new innovations such as collaborative robots, autonomous mobile robots (AMRs), and drones are set to further enhance warehouse operations.

Despite the clear advantages, challenges such as high initial investments, integration complexity, and maintenance requirements remain. However, as technology advances and more companies adopt automated solutions, the future of warehouse robotics is bright. By investing in the right technologies, organizations can create more efficient, flexible, and scalable warehouse operations that are better equipped to meet the demands of the modern supply chain.

Blockchain in Logistics

Blockchain technology, initially popularized by its use in cryptocurrency, has emerged as a transformative tool across various industries, including logistics and supply chain management. In logistics, blockchain offers the potential to improve transparency, enhance security, streamline operations, and provide better traceability of goods and materials. This chapter explores the applications of blockchain in logistics, its benefits in terms of transparency and security, and presents case studies of successful blockchain implementation in the supply chain sector.

1. Applications of Blockchain in the Supply Chain

Blockchain is a decentralized, distributed ledger system that securely records transactions across multiple computers. This technology ensures that once data is recorded, it cannot be altered, creating a permanent and transparent record. The application of blockchain in logistics is vast, encompassing multiple aspects of the supply chain from production to last-mile delivery. Here are several key applications:

1.1 Provenance and Traceability

One of the most significant applications of blockchain in logistics is improving provenance and traceability. Blockchain allows every transaction, movement, and transformation of goods to be recorded in an immutable ledger. For example, it can track the origin of a product, such as raw materials, and follow it through the entire production, storage, and distribution process.

In industries such as food and pharmaceuticals, where provenance and traceability are essential for safety and compliance, blockchain is increasingly used to track products from farm to table or factory to patient. In the event of a food safety issue, blockchain allows for rapid identification of the affected batch, reducing the time and cost of recalls.

1.2 Smart Contracts

Blockchain enables the use of smart contracts, which are self-executing contracts with the terms of the agreement directly written into code. In logistics, smart contracts can automate and enforce agreements between parties. For example, when a shipment reaches its destination, a smart contract can automatically release payment to the supplier or carrier.

Smart contracts reduce the need for intermediaries, improve efficiency, and decrease the potential for disputes or fraud. In addition, they can be used to streamline customs processes, ensuring that the necessary documentation is automatically verified and approved once all the required conditions are met.

1.3 Shipment Tracking and Visibility

Blockchain technology provides real-time visibility into the status of shipments. Sensors placed on goods and vehicles can communicate data to the blockchain, allowing stakeholders to track the location, condition, and status of shipments at every step of the journey. This level of transparency helps improve communication between stakeholders, including manufacturers, shippers, and consumers.

For example, blockchain can track not only the location of a shipment but also environmental data such as temperature, humidity, and shock, which are crucial for the safe delivery of perishable or fragile goods. The transparency provided by blockchain enhances coordination, reduces inefficiencies, and helps avoid delays caused by miscommunication or errors.

1.4 Inventory Management

Blockchain technology can also play a crucial role in inventory management by providing an accurate, real-time record of goods as they move through the supply chain. This reduces the possibility of discrepancies between physical inventory and records, ensuring that companies have accurate data on stock levels. Additionally, by using blockchain to automate inventory tracking, companies can reduce the risks of overstocking or stockouts.

Through blockchain's distributed ledger, all stakeholders have access to the same accurate, up-to-date information about inventory, ensuring better decision-making and operational efficiency. This can lead to improvements in demand forecasting, order fulfillment, and stock management.

1.5 Customs and Cross-Border Trade

Blockchain simplifies customs processes and international trade by providing a secure, transparent, and efficient way to manage trade documentation. Traditionally, customs clearance can be slow, as it requires various forms of documentation and approvals that pass through several intermediaries. Blockchain eliminates many of these bottlenecks by automating and digitizing the documentation process.

For example, when a shipment crosses a border, the relevant data (e.g., product origin, certificates, invoices) is stored on the blockchain and made accessible to customs authorities. Blockchain can also ensure that regulations and tariffs are met by automating the verification process. This reduces the risk of fraud and human error, speeds up the clearance process, and facilitates smoother cross-border trade.

2. Benefits for Transparency and Security

Blockchain offers several advantages in terms of transparency and security that can transform logistics and supply chain management.

2.1 Enhanced Transparency

Blockchain's immutable and decentralized nature ensures that every transaction is recorded and accessible by all parties involved in the supply chain. This creates complete transparency and provides an accurate, real-time history of goods and materials. Stakeholders, including suppliers, manufacturers, shippers, and customers, can access the same information, which helps build trust and accountability.

For example, a consumer purchasing a product can use blockchain to verify the entire supply chain, from the source of raw materials to the final product, ensuring that ethical, environmental, and quality standards are met. This transparency also makes it easier to monitor performance, identify inefficiencies, and resolve disputes.

2.2 Security and Fraud Prevention

Blockchain provides enhanced security through cryptographic encryption. Transactions on the blockchain are secured and linked to previous blocks, creating a chain that cannot be altered. This makes it virtually impossible to manipulate or falsify data, offering an additional layer of security that prevents fraud and counterfeiting.

In logistics, this is particularly important for high-value goods, such as electronics, pharmaceuticals, or luxury items, where the risk of counterfeit products entering the supply chain is significant. Blockchain's tamper-proof nature ensures that the recorded data about the authenticity and condition of the goods is accurate and reliable.

2.3 Reduced Risk of Human Error

The automation provided by blockchain, especially with the use of smart contracts and real-time data sharing, helps minimize human error in supply chain operations. Blockchain can automatically execute transactions when conditions are met, reducing reliance on manual intervention. This leads to fewer mistakes, lower operational costs, and faster processing times.

Additionally, since all participants in the supply chain are working with the same data, there is less room for errors caused by miscommunication or discrepancies between different systems. The consistency and accuracy of blockchain data make it easier to trust the integrity of the supply chain.

2.4 Auditability and Compliance

Blockchain provides a permanent and auditable record of all transactions, allowing companies to easily verify compliance with regulations and industry standards. In sectors like pharmaceuticals, food, and chemicals, where compliance with safety and environmental standards is critical, blockchain offers a reliable way to ensure that all processes meet the necessary requirements.

Companies can also reduce the administrative burden associated with audits, as blockchain's decentralized nature ensures that records are always available and transparent to authorized parties. This is especially useful for supply chains with multiple stakeholders, where tracking compliance can otherwise be complex and time-consuming.

3. Case Studies of Blockchain Implementation in the Supply Chain

Several companies have already implemented blockchain technology to streamline their supply chain operations, offering valuable lessons for others in the industry. Below are a few prominent examples:

3.1 IBM Food Trust Blockchain (Walmart and Nestlé)

One of the most notable implementations of blockchain in logistics is the IBM Food Trust Blockchain, which aims to increase transparency and traceability in the food supply chain. Walmart and Nestlé have both partnered with IBM to use blockchain to track food products from their source to store shelves.

For example, when Walmart wanted to trace the origin of a package of mangoes that had been linked to a foodborne illness outbreak, it used blockchain to track the fruit back to its origin in seconds, a process that would have taken several days using traditional methods. This blockchain-based solution provides transparency to consumers and ensures that food safety standards are met.

3.2 Maersk and IBM TradeLens

Maersk, a global leader in container shipping, has partnered with IBM to create TradeLens, a blockchain-based platform designed to improve the flow of goods through the global supply chain. TradeLens connects various stakeholders, including shipping companies, ports, customs authorities, and logistics providers, enabling real-time tracking of cargo and simplifying the exchange of documentation.

By using blockchain to create a transparent, digital platform, TradeLens eliminates inefficiencies, reduces fraud, and accelerates the process of clearing shipments. The platform also improves collaboration between different stakeholders, leading to more efficient global trade and logistics.

3.3 De Beers and Everledger

De Beers, a global diamond company, uses blockchain to track the provenance of diamonds and prevent the trade of conflict diamonds. Partnering with Everledger, De Beers has implemented a blockchain system that records each diamond's journey from the mine to the consumer. This ensures that diamonds are sourced responsibly and that their origin can be verified at every stage of the supply chain.

Through this blockchain system, De Beers has improved transparency in its supply chain, allowing consumers to trust that the diamonds they purchase are conflict-free. This initiative also helps protect the company's brand reputation and meets the growing consumer demand for ethical sourcing.

Blockchain technology is revolutionizing logistics and supply chain management by enhancing transparency, improving security, and providing real-time traceability of goods. Through applications like smart contracts, shipment tracking, inventory management, and cross-border trade facilitation, blockchain is creating more efficient, secure, and reliable supply chains.

The case studies of IBM's Food Trust Blockchain, Maersk's TradeLens, and De Beers' Everledger highlight the potential of blockchain to solve longstanding challenges in logistics, such as counterfeiting, fraud, and lack of visibility. As blockchain technology continues to mature and gain adoption, it is expected to drive even more innovation in logistics and supply chain management, offering new opportunities for companies to improve their operations, reduce costs, and build trust with consumers.

Sustainable Logistics and Green Practices

Sustainability in logistics and supply chain management has become increasingly important as companies and consumers alike recognize the urgent need to reduce their environmental impact. Logistics operations, including transportation, warehousing, and packaging, contribute significantly to global carbon emissions. As environmental concerns grow, businesses are turning to sustainable logistics practices to reduce their carbon footprint and embrace green technologies. This chapter explores the role of sustainable logistics, focusing on reducing carbon emissions, green warehousing, transportation practices, and the integration of renewable energy in logistics operations.

1. Reducing Carbon Footprint in Logistics

The logistics sector is one of the major contributors to global carbon emissions, primarily due to the reliance on fossil fuels in transportation and the energy consumption associated with warehousing. With rising concerns about climate change and sustainability, reducing the carbon footprint in logistics has become a key priority for companies looking to align their operations with environmental goals and improve long-term sustainability.

1.1 Carbon Emissions in the Logistics Industry

Transportation is the largest contributor to carbon emissions in logistics. The use of diesel trucks, air freight, and ships powered by fossil fuels significantly contributes to greenhouse gas (GHG) emissions. According to the International Transport Forum (ITF), road freight alone accounts for nearly 7% of global CO_2 emissions. In addition, warehousing activities, which often involve energy-intensive heating, cooling, and lighting systems, also contribute to the sector's carbon footprint.

A shift toward sustainable practices is vital not only to meet regulatory requirements but also to appeal to increasingly eco-conscious consumers and stakeholders. Businesses are increasingly aware of the need to balance operational efficiency with environmental responsibility.

1.2 Strategies for Reducing Carbon Footprint

Several strategies are being employed to reduce the carbon footprint of logistics operations:

Optimized Routing and Load Management: Using advanced route planning and fleet management software, logistics companies can minimize the distance traveled, reduce fuel consumption, and lower emissions. Efficient route optimization helps to reduce the time vehicles spend on the road, ensuring trucks are operating at maximum efficiency.

Shift to Alternative Fuels and Electric Vehicles (EVs): Electric trucks, electric forklifts, and vehicles powered by alternative fuels such as hydrogen and natural gas are gaining traction as sustainable alternatives to traditional diesel-powered vehicles. These vehicles have significantly lower emissions and are becoming more cost-competitive as battery technology improves.

Carbon Offsetting: Companies are also investing in carbon offset programs that allow them to compensate for their emissions by funding projects that reduce or capture an equivalent amount of CO_2. Examples include reforestation efforts, renewable energy initiatives, or methane capture projects in landfills.

Carbon Footprint Measurement and Reporting: Businesses are now increasingly adopting carbon footprint measurement tools to track their emissions and identify areas for improvement. By measuring emissions accurately, organizations can set clear targets for reduction and align their operations with global sustainability goals, such as those set by the Paris Agreement.

2. Green Warehousing and Transportation

As part of a broader sustainable logistics strategy, companies are focusing on reducing the environmental impact of their warehousing and transportation operations. Green warehousing and transportation practices aim to reduce energy consumption, lower emissions, and improve the overall environmental performance of logistics operations.

2.1 Green Warehousing

Warehouses are energy-intensive facilities, often requiring large amounts of electricity for lighting, heating, cooling, and refrigeration. Additionally, materials handling equipment such as forklifts and conveyors typically run on fossil fuels, contributing to carbon emissions. However, innovative green warehousing practices are helping companies reduce their energy use and minimize their environmental impact.

Energy-Efficient Building Design: New warehouses are increasingly being built with sustainability in mind. The use of energy-efficient building materials, such as insulated roofing and walls, helps reduce heating and cooling requirements. Large windows and skylights allow for natural lighting, reducing the need for artificial lighting during the day. Green buildings are also often equipped with advanced energy management systems that monitor and optimize energy usage.

Solar Power and Renewable Energy: Many warehouses are now incorporating solar panels and other renewable energy sources into their operations to reduce their reliance on grid electricity. Solar panels on warehouse roofs can generate a significant portion of a building's energy needs, making operations more sustainable and reducing the overall carbon footprint.

Efficient Heating, Ventilation, and Air Conditioning (HVAC) Systems: Advanced HVAC systems that use smart technology can help optimize energy use for heating, cooling, and ventilation. These systems can automatically adjust based on real-time environmental conditions, ensuring that warehouses are energy-efficient while maintaining a comfortable environment for workers and inventory.

Automated Material Handling Systems: Warehouses are increasingly adopting automated systems that require less energy compared to traditional manual systems. Automated guided vehicles (AGVs) and automated storage and retrieval systems (AS/RS) use advanced robotics and AI to improve efficiency, reduce waste, and lower energy consumption in warehouses.

2.2 Green Transportation

Transportation is one of the highest carbon-emitting aspects of logistics, and there is a growing shift toward adopting green practices to minimize environmental impact. Sustainable transportation practices aim to reduce emissions, improve energy efficiency, and use alternative energy sources.

Fuel-Efficient Vehicles: Companies are adopting fuel-efficient vehicles, including trucks and vans that meet or exceed fuel economy standards. Some companies are incorporating hybrid vehicles or electric trucks into their fleets to reduce reliance on fossil fuels. These vehicles generate fewer emissions, lower operational costs, and contribute to long-term sustainability.

Alternative Fuels: The use of alternative fuels, such as biofuels, liquefied natural gas (LNG), and hydrogen, is becoming more prevalent in the transportation sector. These fuels have lower carbon emissions compared to traditional diesel, helping to reduce the overall environmental impact of freight transportation.

Intermodal Transportation: Intermodal transportation involves using a combination of transport modes (e.g., rail, sea, and road) to move goods more efficiently. Rail and sea transport, for example, have much lower emissions per ton-mile than road transportation. By shifting more goods to rail and sea freight, logistics companies can reduce the carbon footprint of their operations while maintaining efficiency and cost-effectiveness.

Last-Mile Delivery Innovations: Last-mile delivery is one of the most carbon-intensive parts of the transportation process. However, several innovations are reducing its environmental impact. These include the use of electric delivery vehicles, cargo bikes, drones, and delivery robots for urban areas. These innovations not only reduce emissions but also improve delivery efficiency, especially in crowded city environments.

3. The Role of Renewable Energy in Logistics

Renewable energy plays a pivotal role in reducing the carbon footprint of logistics operations. As renewable energy sources such as wind, solar, and hydro power become more cost-effective and widely available, their integration into logistics operations is helping to create greener, more sustainable supply chains.

3.1 Solar Energy

Solar energy is one of the most widely adopted renewable energy sources in logistics. Solar panels are commonly installed on warehouse roofs, providing a clean, sustainable source of electricity for warehouse operations. In addition, solar energy can power electric vehicles used in the supply chain, further reducing reliance on fossil fuels.

Companies like Amazon and Walmart are leading the way in installing solar panels across their distribution centers and warehouses. By doing so, they not only reduce their carbon footprint but also generate significant cost savings in energy expenses over time.

3.2 Wind and Hydro Power

Wind and hydro power are also viable renewable energy sources for logistics companies with operations in areas where these resources are abundant. Wind turbines and hydroelectric plants can provide a reliable source of energy, helping companies to offset their reliance on non-renewable energy sources and reduce emissions.

Some companies in Europe have integrated wind energy into their logistics networks, using it to power warehouses or transportation fleets, contributing to a more sustainable logistics model.

3.3 Electric Vehicles Powered by Renewable Energy

The combination of electric vehicles (EVs) and renewable energy is a powerful tool for reducing the environmental impact of logistics operations. Charging stations for electric trucks, vans, and other vehicles are increasingly being powered by renewable energy sources like solar and wind. This closed-loop system ensures that electric vehicles operate on clean energy, further reducing the carbon footprint of the logistics process.

Sustainable logistics and green practices are no longer just a trend but an essential component of modern supply chain management. As companies face mounting pressure from regulators, consumers, and stakeholders to reduce their environmental impact, adopting green logistics practices is becoming a competitive advantage.

By focusing on reducing carbon emissions, improving energy efficiency in warehousing and transportation, and leveraging renewable energy sources, logistics companies can significantly reduce their environmental footprint while enhancing operational efficiency. These practices not only contribute to a cleaner, more sustainable world but also provide long-term cost savings, making them beneficial for both the environment and the bottom line. As sustainable logistics continues to evolve, it will play a critical role in shaping the future of global supply chains.

E-Commerce and Omnichannel Logistics

The rapid growth of e-commerce has transformed logistics operations across the globe. With more consumers turning to online shopping, businesses are increasingly looking for innovative ways to meet customer expectations for fast, efficient, and flexible delivery options. The expansion of e-commerce has led to the rise of omnichannel logistics, a system that integrates different distribution channels—brick-and-mortar stores, online platforms, and third-party providers—into a cohesive network. In this chapter, we will explore the growth of e-commerce logistics, the challenges inherent in omnichannel distribution, and strategies for ensuring seamless integration in the modern supply chain.

1. Growth of E-Commerce Logistics

The growth of e-commerce logistics is directly tied to the surge in online shopping, which has become a dominant force in the global retail market. As of 2023, the global e-commerce market is valued at several trillion dollars and continues to grow year after year, a trend that has only been accelerated by the COVID-19 pandemic. Consumers now expect a wider range of products delivered quickly and conveniently, with same-day or next-day delivery options increasingly becoming the norm.

1.1 The Shift to Online Shopping

E-commerce has not only changed how consumers shop but also where they shop from. With the availability of mobile phones, tablets, and other devices, consumers now have the ability to shop from anywhere at any time, further contributing to the rise in demand for online shopping. This shift has put enormous pressure on logistics networks to adapt quickly and efficiently.

The challenge for businesses is to maintain a fast, reliable service that meets consumer expectations, including easy returns, tracking, and flexible delivery options. E-commerce logistics involves moving goods from the manufacturer or supplier to the consumer's door, often with a higher volume of smaller, more frequent shipments than traditional retail logistics.

1.2 The Role of Technology in E-Commerce Logistics

Technology plays a pivotal role in the growth of e-commerce logistics. Advancements in artificial intelligence (AI), data analytics, and machine learning have enabled companies to optimize their inventory, improve demand forecasting, and automate key processes. These technologies help ensure that the right products are in the right place at the right time, reducing delays and enhancing the overall customer experience.

Additionally, technologies like automated warehouses, drones, and robots are improving efficiency, enabling companies to meet the growing demand for faster delivery times. Real-time tracking and monitoring systems give customers visibility into the status of their orders, enhancing transparency and building trust.

2. Challenges in Omnichannel Distribution

Omnichannel logistics presents a unique set of challenges because it requires companies to manage and integrate multiple distribution channels, both online and offline. These challenges can be complex, as they involve coordinating inventory, shipping, and returns across various sales platforms. The increasing complexity of consumer demands, coupled with the need for real-time visibility, means that businesses must adopt a comprehensive strategy to integrate their logistics networks.

2.1 Inventory Visibility and Management

One of the major challenges in omnichannel logistics is maintaining accurate, real-time inventory visibility across all distribution channels. As businesses expand their reach through online and physical stores, maintaining a single, unified view of inventory becomes more difficult. This lack of visibility can result in stockouts, delays, or excess inventory in one channel while there is demand in another.

For example, a customer may order an item online that appears to be in stock, only for the company to discover that it has already been sold in a physical store. Similarly, products in a physical store may not be visible to online customers, leading to inefficiencies and missed sales opportunities.

To overcome this, businesses must invest in technology like Warehouse Management Systems (WMS) and Enterprise Resource Planning (ERP) software that integrate both online and offline inventory management, allowing for a more holistic view of stock and helping to reduce these challenges.

2.2 Managing Multiple Fulfillment Centers

To meet the growing demand for fast delivery, businesses are increasingly using multiple fulfillment centers. This creates logistical complexities, as each center must be managed independently but integrated into the larger supply chain. A decentralized approach to fulfillment can lead to challenges in synchronizing stock levels, routing orders to the appropriate fulfillment center, and ensuring products are delivered in a timely and cost-efficient manner.

Companies must balance the need for local fulfillment centers to meet customer demand with the operational costs of maintaining these centers. Smaller businesses or those with limited warehouse space may struggle to maintain the infrastructure required to operate multiple fulfillment centers effectively.

2.3 Complexity of Last-Mile Delivery

The last-mile delivery phase, which involves delivering goods from a fulfillment center to the customer's doorstep, is one of the most complex and costly components of e-commerce logistics. The growing demand for faster delivery and the increase in single-item orders has exacerbated this issue. As a result, businesses need to optimize their last-mile delivery network to minimize costs while meeting customer expectations for quick and flexible delivery options.

Challenges include managing multiple delivery partners, navigating congested urban areas, and minimizing delivery costs for individual orders. Companies must also find ways to reduce delivery times and improve delivery reliability, especially in a highly competitive market where customers expect delivery within hours, not days.

3. Strategies for Seamless Integration

To overcome the challenges of omnichannel distribution and improve overall efficiency, businesses must adopt strategies for seamless integration of their logistics networks. These strategies aim to align inventory management, fulfillment processes, transportation, and customer service across all distribution channels.

3.1 Unified Inventory Management

A key strategy for seamless integration is the implementation of unified inventory management. By consolidating inventory data from both brick-and-mortar stores and online platforms, companies can ensure that they have an accurate, real-time view of available stock. This enables businesses to allocate inventory dynamically across channels, reducing the risk of stockouts or excess inventory in any one location.

Using advanced inventory management tools, companies can automate the transfer of stock between warehouses and stores, ensuring that products are available where they are needed most. Additionally, companies can optimize stock levels based on demand forecasts, which is especially important for businesses with a wide range of products.

3.2 Cross-Channel Fulfillment Options

Cross-channel fulfillment allows companies to fulfill customer orders from multiple sources, such as retail stores, distribution centers, or drop-shipping suppliers. This approach ensures that orders can be fulfilled quickly and cost-effectively, regardless of where the products are located. For example, a retailer can ship an online order from a nearby store if that store has the product in stock, reducing shipping times and costs.

To successfully implement cross-channel fulfillment, companies need to ensure that their systems are integrated, allowing them to determine the most efficient fulfillment center based on location, stock levels, and customer preferences.

3.3 Last-Mile Delivery Innovations

To address the challenges of last-mile delivery, businesses are adopting several innovative strategies, including the use of delivery lockers, crowd-sourced delivery services, and smart delivery technologies. Delivery lockers allow customers to pick up their orders at convenient locations, reducing the need for home deliveries and the associated costs. Crowdsourced delivery services, where individuals or drivers provide delivery services, can increase flexibility and speed.

Additionally, technologies like drones, autonomous vehicles, and robotic delivery are gaining traction. These innovations can reduce labor costs, enhance efficiency, and improve delivery speed, all while reducing environmental impact by utilizing electric-powered vehicles.

3.4 Data-Driven Decision Making

Using data analytics to optimize logistics decisions is essential for e-commerce and omnichannel logistics. Businesses can use data from various touchpoints—such as sales history, customer behavior, and delivery patterns—to make informed decisions about inventory management, transportation routes, and fulfillment options.

Predictive analytics can help companies forecast demand, optimize stock levels, and minimize backorders, while real-time data can provide visibility into the status of orders, enabling businesses to proactively address potential issues before they affect the customer experience.

3.5 Customer-Centric Approach

The success of omnichannel logistics ultimately depends on customer satisfaction. Businesses must ensure that their logistics strategies are aligned with customer expectations for fast, flexible, and reliable delivery options. Providing customers with the ability to choose between home delivery, in-store pickup, or even local delivery hubs gives them greater flexibility and enhances the overall shopping experience.

Clear communication about delivery timelines, real-time order tracking, and a simple, hassle-free returns process are critical elements of a customer-centric logistics strategy.

E-commerce and omnichannel logistics are reshaping the way businesses operate and deliver value to customers. The growth of e-commerce has led to the need for sophisticated logistics strategies that integrate various distribution channels and provide seamless, efficient delivery options. While challenges such as inventory visibility, fulfillment center management, and last-mile delivery remain significant, businesses that successfully integrate their logistics networks can create a competitive advantage by providing better service and meeting the ever-growing expectations of consumers.

To achieve success in omnichannel logistics, businesses must invest in advanced technologies, data-driven decision-making, and customer-centric strategies that enable them to deliver fast, reliable, and cost-effective service across all channels. As the logistics landscape continues to evolve, companies that prioritize seamless integration and sustainability will be well-positioned to thrive in the dynamic world of e-commerce.

Section 5: Managing Operations and Risks

Risk Management in Logistics

Logistics and supply chain operations are inherently exposed to a wide range of risks that can disrupt the smooth flow of goods, services, and information. These risks can arise from various sources, including natural disasters, economic shifts, geopolitical tensions, and technological failures. Effective risk management in logistics is essential for ensuring that businesses can continue to operate efficiently and maintain customer satisfaction, even in the face of unforeseen events.

In this chapter, we will explore the process of identifying and assessing risks in logistics, developing contingency plans to mitigate these risks, and managing disruptions within the supply chain. By understanding how to anticipate, prepare for, and respond to risks, businesses can safeguard their operations and improve resilience.

1. Identifying and Assessing Risks

The first step in effective risk management is identifying potential risks. These risks can be classified into several categories, each with its unique characteristics and impacts on logistics operations. Some common types of risks include:

1.1 Operational Risks

Operational risks refer to the internal challenges that companies face in their logistics operations. These include issues such as inventory mismanagement, equipment breakdowns, labor shortages, or delays in manufacturing. Operational risks can be caused by human error, process inefficiencies, or failures in the systems that support logistics activities.

For example, an unexpected shortage of raw materials can delay the production process, leading to a backlog of orders and delays in delivery. Similarly, a breakdown in warehouse equipment, such as conveyor belts or forklifts, can hinder the movement of goods and disrupt order fulfillment.

1.2 External Risks

External risks originate outside the company and are often harder to predict and control. These risks can include natural disasters, such as floods, hurricanes, and earthquakes, or man-made events like political instability, labor strikes, or economic downturns.

For instance, a hurricane that disrupts port operations can delay the arrival of goods from overseas, creating supply chain bottlenecks. Similarly, political unrest in a key supplier country can lead to supply shortages or price increases, impacting the cost and availability of materials.

1.3 Financial Risks

Financial risks relate to the economic factors that can impact the logistics operations. Currency fluctuations, fuel price changes, or shifts in the global economy can all pose financial risks. Rising transportation costs, for example, can increase the cost of delivering goods, which might erode profit margins.

Financial risks can also arise from the creditworthiness of logistics partners, including carriers or suppliers. If a supplier or logistics service provider faces financial difficulties, it could result in delays or disruptions in the supply chain.

1.4 Technological Risks

Technological risks refer to the failure of systems or infrastructure that support logistics operations. These include software malfunctions, cybersecurity breaches, data loss, or disruptions caused by new technological implementations that do not go as planned. With increasing reliance on automation, real-time tracking systems, and AI, businesses are vulnerable to potential system breakdowns.

For example, a cybersecurity attack that compromises a company's order management system could result in significant disruptions, including the loss of sensitive customer information and the inability to process orders.

1.5 Environmental Risks

Environmental risks are becoming increasingly relevant as companies are pressured to adopt more sustainable and eco-friendly practices. Environmental factors such as climate change, pollution, and resource scarcity can directly impact logistics operations. Rising sea levels or frequent natural disasters, like droughts or wildfires, can affect the transportation network, delay shipments, or destroy infrastructure.

In addition, businesses that fail to comply with environmental regulations may face legal risks, fines, or reputational damage. For instance, stricter emissions standards could require companies to invest in more expensive fuel-efficient transportation options.

2. Contingency Planning and Mitigation Strategies

Once risks are identified and assessed, it is crucial to develop contingency plans to mitigate their impact on logistics operations. Contingency planning involves creating alternative courses of action to ensure that business operations can continue even when disruptions occur. The goal is to minimize the impact of a disruption and restore normal operations as quickly as possible.

2.1 Building Resilience into the Supply Chain

To manage risks effectively, businesses need to build resilience into their supply chain. This means designing logistics systems that can quickly adapt to disruptions and continue to function with minimal interruption. Some strategies to enhance supply chain resilience include:

Diversification of Suppliers and Distribution Channels: By sourcing materials and products from multiple suppliers and using various distribution channels, businesses can reduce their dependency on a single source. This approach reduces the risk of complete disruption if one supplier or channel is affected by external events.

Buffer Stock and Safety Inventory: Maintaining buffer stock or safety inventory can act as a cushion in case of disruptions. While keeping extra stock may seem costly, it can prevent stockouts and delays during periods of uncertainty.

Flexible Transportation Networks: Building flexibility into transportation networks allows companies to quickly reroute shipments if necessary. This can involve using multiple transportation modes, leveraging third-party logistics providers (3PLs), and working with multiple carriers to avoid bottlenecks.

2.2 Scenario Planning

Scenario planning involves developing and analyzing various risk scenarios to determine how they might impact logistics operations and what actions need to be taken in each case. This method allows companies to prepare for a range of potential disruptions, from extreme weather events to geopolitical tensions.

For instance, a company could model the potential impact of a major transportation strike or a large-scale natural disaster, estimating the financial and operational consequences of such events. The analysis would help identify vulnerabilities and guide the creation of specific mitigation strategies, such as sourcing from alternative suppliers or increasing inventory for critical products.

2.3 Insurance and Risk Transfer

While it is not possible to eliminate all risks, businesses can transfer some of the financial consequences through insurance. Insurance policies for logistics operations, such as cargo insurance, liability insurance, or business interruption insurance, can help mitigate the financial impact of unforeseen disruptions. This allows businesses to recover faster and reduce their exposure to financial losses.

Additionally, businesses may choose to partner with third-party logistics providers (3PLs) or use outsourcing arrangements as a way to transfer risk. By outsourcing certain logistics functions, such as transportation or warehousing, businesses can transfer operational risks to service providers who have the expertise and resources to handle them effectively.

3. Managing Disruptions in the Supply Chain

Despite the best efforts to identify risks and prepare for potential disruptions, supply chains will inevitably face challenges. How businesses respond to these disruptions can significantly impact the speed of recovery and the long-term sustainability of operations.

3.1 Crisis Management Teams

When a disruption occurs, businesses should have a crisis management team in place to quickly assess the situation and make decisions about how to proceed. These teams are typically cross-functional, including representatives from logistics, procurement, customer service, and IT. Their role is to ensure that the business can respond quickly, minimize the impact on customers, and restore normal operations as efficiently as possible.

3.2 Communication and Transparency

Effective communication during a disruption is critical. Businesses should be transparent with customers, suppliers, and partners about the situation, including the cause of the disruption, the steps being taken to address it, and the expected timeline for resolution. Providing real-time updates through tracking systems and customer service channels helps maintain trust and manage customer expectations.

3.3 Post-Disruption Evaluation and Improvement

After a disruption has been managed and normal operations have resumed, businesses should conduct a post-event evaluation to identify lessons learned. This involves reviewing the effectiveness of the response, identifying areas for improvement, and updating contingency plans accordingly. Continuous improvement is a key component of risk management, as it allows businesses to refine their approach and be better prepared for future disruptions.

Risk management in logistics is essential for maintaining business continuity in an increasingly complex and unpredictable global environment. By identifying and assessing risks, developing contingency plans, and managing disruptions effectively, businesses can minimize the impact of potential disruptions on their supply chains.

Building resilience into logistics operations, adopting scenario planning, and leveraging insurance and risk transfer strategies are critical steps in ensuring that businesses can continue to operate even in the face of unforeseen events. As supply chains become more interconnected and globalized, the ability to respond quickly and effectively to disruptions will remain a key determinant of success in logistics and supply chain management.

Cost Management in Logistics

Effective cost management is one of the most crucial aspects of logistics operations. The ability to manage costs while maintaining service quality directly impacts a company's bottom line and its ability to compete in a globalized and cost-sensitive market. Logistics costs can constitute a significant portion of overall operating expenses, often ranging from 10% to 20% of a company's revenue. As such, understanding the key cost drivers, developing strategies for cost reduction, and balancing costs with service quality are essential for businesses aiming to optimize their logistics operations.

In this chapter, we will explore the key cost drivers in logistics, examine strategies for cost reduction, and discuss how businesses can strike a balance between cost-efficiency and the quality of service they provide.

1. Key Cost Drivers in Logistics Operations

Logistics costs are influenced by a range of factors that directly affect how much a company spends on transportation, warehousing, inventory, and other logistics services. These costs are often categorized into several key areas:

1.1 Transportation Costs

Transportation is typically the largest component of logistics expenses, often accounting for more than half of the total logistics costs. These costs include expenses related to moving goods from suppliers to distribution centers, from warehouses to customers, and among various points in the supply chain. Factors that influence transportation costs include:

Distance: The further goods need to travel, the higher the transportation costs. Long-distance shipments often incur higher fuel charges, road tolls, and vehicle maintenance costs.

Mode of Transport: Different modes of transport (road, rail, air, sea) come with varying cost structures. For example, air freight is faster but more expensive compared to sea freight.

Fuel Costs: Fluctuations in fuel prices directly impact transportation costs, especially for businesses that rely heavily on road or air transportation.

Freight Rates: Shipping rates charged by carriers or logistics providers can vary depending on factors like shipment size, weight, and timing.

1.2 Inventory Management Costs

Inventory management costs represent another significant portion of logistics expenses. These costs include:

Holding Costs: The costs associated with storing inventory in warehouses, such as rent, utilities, insurance, and labor. Higher inventory levels result in higher holding costs.

Stockouts and Backorders: The costs of stockouts can include lost sales, customer dissatisfaction, and expedited shipping charges when an out-of-stock item needs to be replenished quickly.

Inventory Obsolescence: In certain industries, products can become obsolete or perishable, leading to write-offs or markdowns.

1.3 Warehousing Costs

Warehousing costs are incurred for storing, handling, and managing inventory in distribution centers or warehouses. These costs include:

Storage Space: The cost of renting or owning warehouse space, which is typically measured by the square footage.

Labor: Costs related to the employees involved in receiving, storing, picking, packing, and shipping inventory.

Material Handling: The costs associated with equipment like forklifts, conveyors, and storage systems.

Technology: Investments in warehouse management systems (WMS), automation, and other technological tools also contribute to warehousing costs.

1.4 Packaging Costs

Packaging is another cost driver in logistics, impacting both transportation and warehousing. Packaging costs include the materials used to pack and protect products during transit, such as boxes, bubble wrap, pallets, and shrink wrap. Additionally, improper packaging can lead to damage during transportation, resulting in higher costs due to returns or replacements.

1.5 Administration and Overhead Costs

Administrative costs are often hidden but can contribute significantly to logistics expenses. These costs include:

Planning and Coordination: The costs associated with logistics planning, order processing, and coordination among suppliers, carriers, and customers.

Technology and IT Systems: Investments in logistics management software, data analytics, and communication tools to improve the visibility and efficiency of operations.

Compliance Costs: Regulatory compliance and documentation (such as customs duties and taxes) can also add to logistics costs, especially for international shipments.

2. Strategies for Cost Reduction in Logistics

Once the key cost drivers are identified, companies can implement several strategies to reduce logistics expenses. These strategies involve optimizing processes, leveraging technology, and making smarter decisions across the supply chain.

2.1 Optimizing Transportation Networks

One of the most effective ways to reduce transportation costs is by optimizing the transportation network. Companies can use various strategies to improve efficiency and reduce costs:

Consolidation of Shipments: By consolidating smaller shipments into larger ones, companies can take advantage of economies of scale. Less-than-truckload (LTL) and full-truckload (FTL) shipping methods can help optimize load utilization.

Route Optimization: Using advanced route planning software helps identify the most efficient delivery routes, reducing fuel consumption and transportation time.

Negotiating Freight Rates: Companies can negotiate better rates with carriers based on volume, frequency of shipments, and long-term contracts. Partnering with third-party logistics providers (3PLs) may also provide cost-saving opportunities.

2.2 Lean Inventory Management

Lean inventory management focuses on reducing inventory levels while ensuring that products are available when needed. Strategies for lean inventory management include:

Just-in-Time (JIT) Inventory: By coordinating with suppliers to deliver goods only when needed, companies can minimize holding costs and reduce inventory levels.

Demand Forecasting: Advanced forecasting techniques help predict demand more accurately, reducing the risk of overstocking or understocking.

Cross-Docking: Cross-docking allows for the direct transfer of goods from inbound to outbound transportation without being stored in the warehouse, reducing handling and storage costs.

2.3 Warehousing Optimization

Reducing warehousing costs involves improving the layout, design, and efficiency of warehouse operations. Several strategies to optimize warehousing include:

Warehouse Layout Optimization: Analyzing and redesigning the warehouse layout to reduce unnecessary movements, improve picking efficiency, and streamline the flow of goods.

Automation: Implementing automated systems for inventory tracking, picking, and packing can improve efficiency and reduce labor costs.

Outsourcing: Some companies may benefit from outsourcing warehousing functions to third-party providers (3PLs) who can offer better economies of scale.

2.4 Technology Integration

Investing in technology is a long-term strategy for reducing logistics costs. Key technologies include:

Warehouse Management Systems (WMS): WMS helps optimize inventory management, reduce stockouts, and improve picking and packing efficiency.

Transportation Management Systems (TMS): TMS helps with route optimization, carrier management, and freight auditing, ensuring that transportation costs are minimized.

Automated Tracking and Monitoring: Real-time tracking systems allow for better visibility and proactive management of logistics operations, reducing delays and costly disruptions.

2.5 Packaging Optimization

Improper or excessive packaging can lead to higher transportation and storage costs. Companies can reduce packaging costs by:

Standardizing Packaging: Using standard-sized boxes or containers that can accommodate multiple products helps reduce packaging waste and costs.

Reducing Packaging Materials: Using lighter or more durable materials can reduce packaging costs without compromising product protection.

Package Optimization: Optimizing the size and weight of packages to fit transportation requirements can reduce shipping costs, especially in air and sea freight.

3. Balancing Costs with Service Quality

While cost reduction is essential, it is equally important not to compromise service quality, as customer satisfaction is often linked to the efficiency and reliability of logistics operations. Balancing costs with service quality requires a strategic approach:

3.1 Prioritizing Service Levels

To strike the right balance, businesses must define service level expectations for different types of products and customers. For example, high-value or perishable products may require faster shipping, which may incur higher transportation costs, while less time-sensitive products can be delivered through more cost-effective methods.

3.2 Cost-to-Serve Analysis

A cost-to-serve analysis helps businesses understand the full cost of serving different customer segments, including transportation, inventory, and warehousing. By identifying the most profitable customers or product lines, businesses can focus on providing the best service to those segments without overspending on lower-margin customers.

3.3 Continuous Improvement and Monitoring

Regular monitoring of logistics performance is crucial for balancing cost and service. Key performance indicators (KPIs) such as on-time delivery, order accuracy, and transportation costs per unit can help assess the effectiveness of cost-saving initiatives while ensuring that service quality is maintained.

Cost management in logistics is a multifaceted challenge that requires businesses to balance cost-saving measures with the need to provide excellent service to customers. By understanding key cost drivers, implementing cost reduction strategies, and optimizing logistics operations, businesses can achieve significant cost savings without compromising on service quality. The key to success is adopting a holistic approach that integrates transportation, inventory management, warehousing, and technology to create an efficient and cost-effective logistics system that meets customer expectations.

Global Logistics and Trade Compliance

Global logistics plays a pivotal role in today's interconnected world, enabling the flow of goods across countries and continents. However, with the expansion of global trade comes the complexity of navigating diverse regulations, managing risks, and ensuring that operations are compliant with local and international laws. Effective global logistics management requires businesses to address the challenges of international logistics, understand customs regulations and trade agreements, and efficiently manage cross-border logistics to ensure smooth operations.

In this chapter, we will explore the challenges of international logistics, the importance of understanding customs regulations and trade agreements, and the best practices for managing cross-border logistics effectively.

1. Challenges of International Logistics

Managing international logistics presents several unique challenges that businesses must address to optimize the global supply chain. These challenges are multifaceted and require careful planning, coordination, and expertise to overcome.

1.1 Geopolitical Risks

Geopolitical risks, including political instability, trade wars, and shifting government policies, can significantly disrupt international logistics. Changes in trade policies or the imposition of tariffs, for example, can affect the cost and feasibility of international shipments. Companies must be agile in their logistics strategies, staying informed about global political changes and adjusting operations as needed.

1.2 Complex Regulations and Compliance Requirements

International logistics is subject to an array of complex regulations that differ from country to country. These regulations often include:

Import and export regulations: Each country has its own set of rules governing the import and export of goods. These regulations may include tariffs, quotas, and restrictions on certain types of goods.

Customs duties and taxes: Customs duties are taxes imposed on imports and exports, and these can vary greatly depending on the type of product and the destination country.

Sanctions and embargoes: Some countries impose trade sanctions or embargoes on specific nations or entities, further complicating cross-border logistics operations.

Environmental regulations: Many countries have specific environmental regulations, including restrictions on packaging materials, emissions, and the disposal of hazardous goods.

Managing compliance across various jurisdictions is a significant challenge for global logistics managers. Non-compliance can lead to delays, fines, and damage to a company's reputation.

1.3 Currency Fluctuations

Currency fluctuations are another challenge faced by businesses involved in international logistics. Exchange rate volatility can impact the cost of goods and services, particularly for businesses dealing with suppliers or customers in different currencies. Price fluctuations can be unpredictable, making it difficult to forecast costs and manage pricing structures. Companies must have strategies in place to mitigate the impact of currency risks, such as hedging or working with local suppliers in specific regions.

1.4 Transportation and Infrastructure Issues

International logistics often involves multiple modes of transportation, such as air, sea, and land. However, each mode has its own set of challenges, including:

Capacity constraints: Limited availability of transport capacity, especially during peak seasons, can lead to delays and higher costs.

Infrastructure quality: The state of infrastructure such as ports, roads, and rail systems can vary greatly from country to country. Poor infrastructure can lead to delays, increased costs, and damaged goods.

Cross-border logistics coordination: Coordinating shipments across borders requires managing various logistics partners, customs brokers, freight forwarders, and regulatory authorities, making the process complex and prone to errors.

1.5 Supply Chain Visibility

A lack of visibility across the supply chain is a significant issue in global logistics. Tracking goods in real-time and coordinating multiple parties involved in cross-border shipments can be challenging. Disruptions caused by customs clearance delays, transportation issues, or unforeseen events (such as natural disasters) can go undetected, resulting in increased risks and longer lead times. To maintain smooth operations, businesses need to invest in technology that enhances supply chain visibility, such as real-time tracking systems and predictive analytics.

2. Understanding Customs Regulations and Trade Agreements

Customs regulations and trade agreements are central to the smooth operation of international logistics. These regulations govern the import and export of goods across borders, and understanding them is crucial for ensuring compliance and avoiding delays or penalties.

2.1 Customs Regulations

Customs regulations are the set of rules that govern the import and export of goods between countries. They ensure that goods meet the required safety, quality, and environmental standards, and that the appropriate tariffs and taxes are paid. These regulations may include:

Tariffs and duties: Customs duties are taxes levied on goods when they cross international borders. The rate of duty depends on the type of goods, their value, and their country of origin.

Product classifications: Different countries use specific systems, such as the Harmonized System (HS), to classify products. Accurate product classification is crucial to ensure that goods are correctly taxed and meet regulatory standards.

Documentation requirements: Customs authorities often require a range of documents to clear goods for import or export. These can include invoices, certificates of origin, bills of lading, and packing lists.

Customs inspections: Goods may be subject to inspection by customs authorities to ensure they comply with national regulations, including safety, health, and environmental standards.

Understanding the customs requirements of both the exporting and importing countries is vital for companies engaged in international trade. Working closely with customs brokers and leveraging technology to automate the documentation process can help ensure compliance.

2.2 Trade Agreements

Trade agreements between countries play a significant role in shaping the flow of goods across borders. These agreements can reduce or eliminate tariffs, provide better access to foreign markets, and harmonize regulations. Examples of major trade agreements include:

North American Free Trade Agreement (NAFTA): A trade agreement between Canada, Mexico, and the United States that aims to reduce trade barriers and facilitate the flow of goods across borders.

European Union (EU) Trade Agreements: The EU has negotiated several free trade agreements with non-EU countries, allowing goods to be traded freely between member states and partner countries.

World Trade Organization (WTO) Agreements: The WTO oversees global trade rules and facilitates trade negotiations among member countries.

By understanding the trade agreements in place between countries, businesses can take advantage of preferential treatment and avoid unnecessary tariffs or import/export restrictions.

3. Managing Cross-Border Logistics Effectively

Managing cross-border logistics involves coordinating the movement of goods across borders while ensuring compliance with customs regulations and minimizing costs. The complexity of international logistics means that businesses must develop robust strategies to manage this process efficiently.

3.1 Selecting the Right Logistics Partners

One of the keys to successful cross-border logistics is selecting the right logistics partners. This includes freight forwarders, customs brokers, and third-party logistics providers (3PLs) that can navigate the complexities of international shipping. These partners should have expertise in handling customs regulations, managing international shipments, and ensuring timely delivery.

Freight Forwarders: Freight forwarders act as intermediaries between businesses and transportation carriers. They can help select the best transportation routes, manage documentation, and ensure compliance with customs regulations.

Customs Brokers: Customs brokers help businesses navigate the customs clearance process by ensuring that goods are properly classified, documented, and cleared through customs.

Third-Party Logistics Providers (3PLs): 3PLs can offer end-to-end logistics services, including warehousing, transportation, and customs clearance, allowing businesses to outsource the complexities of cross-border logistics.

3.2 Streamlining Customs Clearance

Customs clearance can be a bottleneck in cross-border logistics, especially when the process is slow or complicated. Streamlining customs clearance can reduce delays and minimize the risk of fines or penalties. Best practices for managing customs clearance include:

Pre-arranging documentation: Ensuring that all necessary documents are prepared in advance can help avoid delays at the border. This includes invoices, certificates of origin, and any specific certifications required by the importing country.

Automating the process: Automation tools and digital platforms can help speed up the customs clearance process by allowing businesses to submit documents electronically and track the status of shipments in real-time.

Working with experienced customs brokers: Engaging an experienced customs broker can help ensure compliance with regulations and expedite the clearance process.

3.3 Technology in Cross-Border Logistics

Technology plays a crucial role in enhancing the efficiency of cross-border logistics. Technologies such as real-time tracking, blockchain, and cloud-based supply chain management systems can provide businesses with greater visibility into international shipments, automate the documentation process, and ensure compliance with customs regulations.

Real-Time Tracking: Tracking technologies allow businesses to monitor the status of shipments as they move across borders. Real-time tracking can help identify potential delays and allow for proactive problem-solving.

Blockchain: Blockchain technology provides a secure, transparent, and immutable record of transactions. It can help streamline the flow of goods across borders by providing greater visibility and security in customs processes.

Cloud-Based Platforms: Cloud-based logistics platforms enable businesses to share data and collaborate with suppliers, partners, and customs authorities. These platforms improve transparency, reduce errors, and speed up decision-making.

3.4 Risk Mitigation Strategies

Cross-border logistics involves significant risks, including delays, cargo damage, theft, and political instability. To mitigate these risks, businesses should:

Diversify transportation routes: Using multiple transportation routes can help reduce the risk of disruptions caused by geopolitical tensions or natural disasters.

Ensure adequate insurance: Businesses should ensure that their goods are adequately insured for transit, covering risks such as theft, damage, and delays.

Develop contingency plans: Having contingency plans in place for unforeseen events such as border closures or strikes can help minimize the impact of disruptions.

Managing global logistics and ensuring compliance with trade regulations requires a deep understanding of international trade practices, customs regulations, and the complexities of cross-border supply chains. By addressing the challenges of international logistics, leveraging trade agreements, and developing effective strategies for managing cross-border logistics, businesses can streamline operations, reduce risks, and improve efficiency.

In today's competitive global marketplace, businesses that successfully manage their global logistics operations will be better positioned to succeed and capitalize on opportunities in international markets.

Human Resources in Logistics

Human resources (HR) play a critical role in logistics operations, as the efficiency of supply chains and distribution systems depends largely on the skills, training, and motivation of the workforce. The logistics industry encompasses a wide range of roles, from drivers and warehouse workers to supply chain managers and logistics coordinators, all of whom must be properly trained and managed to ensure smooth and effective operations. In this chapter, we explore the key aspects of workforce planning and training in logistics, the role of leadership in logistics management, and the importance of safety and compliance in logistics operations.

1. Workforce Planning and Training

Effective workforce planning and training are foundational to the success of logistics operations. Logistics managers must ensure that the right people with the right skills are in the right positions at the right time. Given the dynamic nature of logistics, which is influenced by seasonal demand fluctuations, transportation needs, and technology changes, workforce planning is a critical component of overall logistics management.

1.1 Workforce Planning in Logistics

Workforce planning involves forecasting the human resources needed for various logistics functions and ensuring that these resources are available when required. A logistics company must have a workforce that is flexible and scalable to meet changing demand, and it must address both short-term and long-term needs.

Demand Forecasting: By analyzing historical data and understanding market trends, logistics managers can forecast future workforce requirements, allowing them to plan staffing levels for busy periods, such as peak seasons or sales promotions.

Labor Flexibility: Logistics managers must build a workforce that can quickly adapt to changing demands. This includes having temporary or seasonal workers available during peak periods, as well as ensuring that full-time staff have cross-functional skills to move between different logistics functions.

Labor Cost Management: The cost of labor can account for a significant portion of logistics expenses. Effective workforce planning helps businesses optimize staffing levels, ensuring that the right number of workers are deployed at the right times, without overstaffing or understaffing.

1.2 Training and Development in Logistics

Training is critical to ensuring that the workforce is capable of meeting the demands of logistics operations. Continuous training programs help employees enhance their skills, stay up-to-date with industry trends, and improve their overall performance.

Skills Development: In logistics, workers must be proficient in a variety of skills, including operating forklifts, understanding inventory management systems, using warehouse management software, and complying with safety regulations. Regular training ensures that employees maintain and improve their skills.

Technological Training: As logistics increasingly relies on automation, artificial intelligence (AI), and robotics, workforce training must also include exposure to new technologies. For instance, workers should be trained in the use of warehouse automation systems, drones, and tracking software to improve operational efficiency.

Soft Skills Training: In addition to technical skills, employees in logistics must also be trained in communication, problem-solving, time management, and leadership. These soft skills are crucial in ensuring efficient collaboration across the supply chain and in delivering excellent customer service.

Effective training programs not only enhance the skills of the workforce but also improve employee satisfaction and retention. Employees who feel that they are being invested in and developed are more likely to stay with the company and contribute to its success.

2. Role of Leadership in Logistics Management

Leadership in logistics management is essential for setting strategic direction, motivating the workforce, and ensuring that operations run smoothly. A strong leadership team can inspire employees, streamline logistics processes, and drive improvements across the organization.

2.1 Strategic Direction and Decision-Making

Leaders in logistics are responsible for setting the overall strategy for operations, which includes selecting the right technologies, designing efficient logistics networks, and ensuring that key performance indicators (KPIs) are met. Effective leadership ensures that logistics operations align with the broader organizational goals and objectives.

Vision and Planning: Logistics leaders must have a clear vision of where the company wants to go and how logistics can support that vision. They need to develop strategies that optimize inventory, streamline transportation, and improve warehouse operations to meet the company's goals.

Data-Driven Decision-Making: Logistics leaders must make decisions based on real-time data and analytics. For instance, leaders need to assess transportation costs, inventory turnover rates, and employee performance metrics to make informed decisions that enhance operational efficiency.

Collaboration Across Departments: Logistics leaders must collaborate with other departments within the organization, such as sales, procurement, and finance, to ensure that logistics decisions align with the company's overall strategy.

2.2 Motivating and Inspiring the Workforce

Effective leadership is key to motivating employees, fostering a positive work culture, and encouraging high performance. In logistics, employees often face challenging working conditions, including long hours, tight deadlines, and physically demanding tasks. A strong leader can help to create an environment where employees are motivated, engaged, and committed to the organization's success.

Recognition and Rewards: Recognizing employees for their hard work and achievements is a key aspect of motivating a logistics workforce. Leaders should establish reward programs, such as performance bonuses, employee of the month awards, and other incentives, to acknowledge outstanding contributions.

Providing Opportunities for Advancement: Leadership should provide employees with opportunities for career development and growth. Offering promotions, cross-training opportunities, and mentorship programs can help employees feel valued and engaged.

Creating a Positive Work Culture: Logistics leaders should strive to create a work environment that values safety, teamwork, and respect. This kind of environment fosters loyalty and increases employee retention.

2.3 Building Resilience in the Logistics Team

Leadership in logistics is not only about managing day-to-day operations but also about preparing the workforce to handle disruptions. Logistics operations are vulnerable to various risks, such as natural disasters, strikes, and supply chain disruptions. Leaders must help employees build resilience to handle these challenges.

Crisis Management: Logistics leaders must have contingency plans in place for dealing with disruptions. This includes training employees to respond effectively to emergencies, whether they are related to transportation delays, system outages, or supply chain interruptions.

Promoting a Problem-Solving Mindset: Effective leaders encourage employees to think critically and solve problems creatively. By fostering a proactive and solutions-oriented mindset, logistics leaders can improve operational efficiency and reduce downtime during disruptions.

3. Safety and Compliance in Logistics Operations

Ensuring safety and compliance in logistics operations is a primary responsibility for HR and management teams. Logistics environments, such as warehouses and transportation fleets, can be hazardous, and non-compliance with regulations can lead to accidents, legal penalties, and damage to a company's reputation.

3.1 Safety in Logistics

Safety is a top priority in logistics, as workers are often exposed to physical risks, such as heavy lifting, operating machinery, and working in high-risk environments. Ensuring that safety protocols are in place can help reduce accidents and improve overall employee well-being.

Training for Safety: All logistics employees should receive regular safety training to understand the risks associated with their roles and how to mitigate them. This includes training on the safe use of equipment, handling hazardous materials, and emergency procedures.

Personal Protective Equipment (PPE): Providing employees with the necessary PPE—such as gloves, helmets, safety vests, and steel-toed boots—is essential for minimizing workplace injuries.

Warehouse Safety: In warehouse settings, safety measures such as clear signage, proper storage techniques, and regular equipment maintenance should be in place to prevent accidents and injuries.

3.2 Compliance with Regulations

Logistics operations are subject to numerous regulations, ranging from labor laws to environmental standards. Ensuring compliance with these regulations is essential to avoid penalties and legal issues.

Labor Law Compliance: Companies must adhere to labor laws regarding wages, working hours, and employee rights. Failure to comply with these laws can result in legal action and fines.

Environmental Compliance: Logistics companies must also comply with environmental regulations, such as those related to waste disposal, emissions, and packaging materials. Non-compliance can result in fines and damage to a company's reputation.

Customs and Trade Compliance: Logistics managers must ensure that their operations comply with customs regulations when shipping goods internationally. This includes ensuring that proper documentation is in place and that goods meet the required standards for export or import.

3.3 Promoting a Safety Culture

A safety culture should be ingrained in the organization's values and practices. Leadership plays a crucial role in creating and maintaining this culture by emphasizing the importance of safety at all levels of the organization.

Continuous Safety Improvement: Safety practices should be continuously reviewed and improved based on feedback from employees and safety audits. This includes identifying new risks, implementing new safety technologies, and adjusting policies as needed.

Employee Involvement in Safety: Engaging employees in safety programs and encouraging them to report hazards can help create a culture of accountability. Employees who are actively involved in safety initiatives are more likely to follow procedures and stay alert to potential risks.

Human resources in logistics are essential for the success of supply chain operations. Workforce planning and training ensure that logistics companies have the right people with the right skills in place to meet operational demands. Strong leadership helps guide logistics teams, drive strategic decision-making, and foster a positive work culture. Ensuring safety and compliance is not just a regulatory requirement but also a moral responsibility to protect employees and ensure smooth operations. By investing in their workforce and maintaining high standards of safety and compliance, logistics companies can achieve greater efficiency, reduce risks, and enhance employee satisfaction.

Section 6: Future Trends and Case Studies

Future Trends in Logistics and Distribution

The logistics and distribution industry is undergoing a rapid transformation due to emerging technologies, evolving consumer demands, and global economic shifts. The future of logistics will be marked by increased automation, greater efficiency, and improved customer experiences. To stay competitive, companies must adapt to these changes and proactively prepare for future challenges. In this section, we will explore emerging technologies that are reshaping logistics, the role of artificial intelligence (AI) and machine learning, and strategies for preparing for future challenges in logistics and distribution.

1.1 Emerging Technologies and Their Impact

Technological advancements are revolutionizing the logistics and distribution industry, making it possible to streamline operations, enhance efficiency, and deliver a better customer experience. These technologies have the potential to change how goods are transported, stored, and delivered. Some of the most notable emerging technologies in logistics include:

1.1.1 Internet of Things (IoT)

The Internet of Things (IoT) refers to the network of interconnected devices that communicate with each other and transmit data. In logistics, IoT devices are being used to track inventory, monitor the condition of goods in transit, and optimize warehouse operations.

Smart Sensors: IoT-enabled sensors can monitor temperature, humidity, and other environmental factors in real-time, ensuring that sensitive products (such as perishable goods or pharmaceuticals) are transported under optimal conditions.

Inventory Tracking: RFID (Radio Frequency Identification) and GPS systems allow companies to track goods throughout the entire supply chain, offering real-time visibility and reducing inventory errors or theft.

Predictive Maintenance: IoT devices embedded in trucks and warehouses can provide real-time data on equipment performance, alerting companies to maintenance needs before they cause downtime.

1.1.2 Autonomous Vehicles and Drones

The use of autonomous vehicles and drones is rapidly gaining traction in logistics. These technologies are expected to reduce human labor, increase delivery speed, and cut costs.

Autonomous Trucks: Self-driving trucks can revolutionize long-haul transportation by reducing the need for drivers and enabling 24/7 operation. These trucks can also optimize routes in real-time, reducing fuel consumption and improving delivery efficiency.

Delivery Drones: Drones can be used for last-mile delivery, providing faster and more flexible options for small, lightweight shipments. Drones can bypass traffic congestion and deliver packages to remote or urban areas quickly, improving customer satisfaction.

1.1.3 Blockchain Technology

Blockchain offers a secure and transparent way to track transactions across the supply chain. By providing an immutable record of every transaction, blockchain technology can improve traceability, security, and efficiency in logistics.

Smart Contracts: Blockchain enables the use of smart contracts, which automatically execute and enforce the terms of an agreement when certain conditions are met. In logistics, smart contracts can streamline processes such as customs clearance, payment processing, and supply chain traceability.

Transparency and Security: Blockchain can enhance visibility and trust in the supply chain, reducing fraud, errors, and the need for intermediaries.

1.1.4 Augmented Reality (AR) and Virtual Reality (VR)

Augmented Reality (AR) and Virtual Reality (VR) are becoming increasingly important in logistics, especially in warehouses and distribution centers.

Warehouse Operations: AR technology can help workers navigate warehouses by overlaying digital information on their environment. For example, workers can receive visual cues on the optimal path to pick items or receive real-time inventory updates.

Training and Simulation: VR can be used to simulate warehouse environments for training purposes, allowing employees to practice operating machinery and performing tasks in a safe, controlled setting before engaging in real-world operations.

1.2 Role of AI and Machine Learning in Logistics

Artificial intelligence (AI) and machine learning (ML) are becoming integral to logistics operations. These technologies enable companies to automate tasks, optimize operations, and improve decision-making. AI and ML can be used across a variety of logistics functions, including transportation, inventory management, demand forecasting, and customer service.

1.2.1 Predictive Analytics for Demand Forecasting

AI and machine learning models can analyze historical data, customer behavior, and market trends to predict future demand. This enables companies to optimize inventory levels, avoid stockouts or overstock situations, and reduce supply chain inefficiencies.

Inventory Optimization: AI algorithms can help companies maintain the right stock levels, reducing the risk of stockouts or excess inventory. Machine learning models can adjust inventory predictions based on real-time data, improving forecasting accuracy.

Dynamic Pricing: Machine learning models can analyze competitor pricing, demand fluctuations, and customer preferences to optimize pricing strategies and improve profitability.

1.2.2 Automated Warehouse Operations

AI-powered robots and automated systems are transforming warehouse operations. Robots can assist in picking, sorting, and packing items, reducing human labor costs and increasing efficiency.

Robotic Process Automation (RPA): AI-driven robots can work alongside human workers in warehouses to perform repetitive tasks such as picking and sorting, increasing throughput and reducing errors.

Autonomous Forklifts: Autonomous forklifts equipped with AI and IoT capabilities can move goods around the warehouse without human intervention, improving warehouse productivity and safety.

1.2.3 AI-Driven Transportation Optimization

AI is playing an increasingly important role in optimizing transportation routes and managing fleets. AI algorithms can analyze traffic patterns, weather conditions, and real-time data to select the most efficient routes for delivery vehicles.

Route Optimization: AI systems can dynamically adjust delivery routes based on factors such as traffic, weather, and road conditions, reducing delays and improving fuel efficiency.

Fleet Management: AI-powered fleet management systems can track vehicle performance, predict maintenance needs, and optimize fleet utilization, reducing costs and improving operational efficiency.

1.3 Preparing for Future Challenges in Logistics

As logistics and distribution systems continue to evolve, businesses must be proactive in addressing the challenges that arise. The key to success in the future of logistics will be the ability to adapt quickly to change and leverage emerging technologies to stay competitive. To prepare for future challenges, logistics companies must focus on the following strategies:

1.3.1 Agility and Flexibility

In an increasingly volatile global market, logistics companies must be agile and flexible in their operations. This involves the ability to quickly adapt to changes in demand, disruptions in supply chains, and shifts in consumer behavior.

Scenario Planning: Companies should engage in scenario planning exercises to prepare for various disruptions, such as natural disasters, strikes, or global supply chain disruptions. These plans will enable businesses to respond effectively when faced with unexpected challenges.

Flexible Supply Chain Networks: Logistics companies should develop flexible supply chain networks that can easily be scaled up or down based on changing market conditions. This includes diversifying suppliers and transportation routes to reduce risk.

1.3.2 Sustainability and Green Logistics

Sustainability is becoming a key priority in logistics. Companies must adopt green practices to reduce their carbon footprint and meet regulatory requirements. This includes optimizing transportation routes to reduce fuel consumption, investing in energy-efficient warehouses, and using sustainable packaging materials.

Carbon Emissions Reduction: Logistics companies can reduce their carbon footprint by implementing green technologies, such as electric trucks, solar-powered warehouses, and fuel-efficient transportation systems.

Circular Economy: Embracing a circular economy approach can help logistics companies reduce waste, promote recycling, and maximize the lifecycle value of products.

1.3.3 Talent Management and Workforce Development

As logistics operations become more complex and technology-driven, there is an increasing demand for a skilled workforce. Companies must invest in workforce development, training, and talent retention strategies to ensure that they have the right talent to navigate future challenges.

Upskilling and Reskilling: Logistics companies should invest in upskilling and reskilling programs to equip employees with the necessary skills to operate new technologies and adapt to changes in the industry.

Attracting Talent: To meet the growing demand for skilled workers, logistics companies should focus on attracting top talent by offering competitive compensation packages, professional development opportunities, and a positive work culture.

The future of logistics and distribution will be shaped by emerging technologies, including AI, IoT, autonomous vehicles, and blockchain. These innovations will enhance operational efficiency, reduce costs, and improve customer satisfaction. However, to fully capitalize on these advancements, logistics companies must be prepared to address future challenges, such as workforce development, sustainability, and global supply chain risks. By embracing these trends and proactively adapting to the evolving logistics landscape, companies can maintain a competitive edge and thrive in an increasingly dynamic global market.

Case Studies in Logistics Excellence

Logistics excellence is often the result of a well-planned strategy, consistent execution, and the use of innovative technologies. Many industry leaders have perfected their logistics operations to gain competitive advantages in the marketplace. By studying real-world examples, we can uncover valuable lessons that organizations can apply to optimize their logistics operations. In this section, we will explore successful logistics strategies from some of the world's top companies and identify key takeaways that can be implemented in other organizations.

1.1 Successful Logistics Strategies from Industry Leaders

1.1.1 Amazon: Mastering E-commerce Logistics

Amazon is often regarded as one of the best examples of logistics excellence, with its innovative supply chain management systems and customer-centric approach. The company's logistics strategy is built around speed, flexibility, and scalability.

Prime Delivery: Amazon's Prime membership program offers fast and often same-day delivery, which is made possible through the company's vast network of fulfillment centers, regional distribution hubs, and last-mile delivery solutions. By locating fulfillment centers near key metropolitan areas and optimizing inventory management, Amazon can provide faster shipping times and reduce delivery costs.

Technology and Automation: Amazon has heavily invested in technology and automation, particularly in its warehouses. The company uses advanced robotics (e.g., Kiva robots) for sorting, picking, and moving inventory, significantly improving warehouse efficiency and reducing human labor costs. Additionally, Amazon's use of AI and machine learning allows for dynamic inventory management, helping optimize stock levels and forecasting demand.

Last-Mile Delivery: To further reduce delivery times, Amazon has developed its own delivery network, including Amazon Flex (a program where individuals use their own vehicles to deliver packages) and a fleet of drones for potential future use. The company also partners with third-party logistics providers to ensure that it can reach customers more efficiently.

Key Takeaways:

Invest in technology to optimize warehouse management and improve operational efficiency.

Prioritize customer satisfaction by providing fast and reliable delivery options.

Build a flexible and scalable logistics network to handle demand fluctuations.

1.1.2 Walmart: Efficient Inventory Management and Global Supply Chain

Walmart is another prime example of logistics excellence, particularly in terms of inventory management and supply chain efficiency. With thousands of stores worldwide and a vast supply chain, Walmart has become a leader in operational efficiency.

Cross-Docking and Inventory Management: One of Walmart's standout logistics strategies is cross-docking, a method where products are directly transferred from inbound trucks to outbound trucks, minimizing storage time. This system reduces inventory holding costs and improves the speed of distribution. Walmart also uses a Just-in-Time (JIT) inventory system to maintain optimal stock levels without excess inventory.

Global Supply Chain Network: Walmart has built a massive supply chain network with a mix of centralized and decentralized distribution centers. It also utilizes sophisticated technology for demand forecasting, ensuring that products are available at the right place and time without overstocking.

Vendor Partnerships: Walmart's relationships with suppliers are essential to its logistics success. By using a "Retail Link" system, suppliers can access real-time data on inventory levels, orders, and sales forecasts. This collaboration allows for more accurate demand forecasting and ensures that the right products are delivered to stores when needed.

Key Takeaways:

Utilize cross-docking to reduce inventory holding costs and improve distribution speed.

Leverage technology for real-time data exchange with suppliers and demand forecasting.

Build a global supply chain network with centralized and decentralized elements for flexibility.

1.1.3 Apple: Streamlined Supply Chain with Focus on Quality and Speed

Apple's logistics strategy focuses on creating an efficient, high-quality, and cost-effective supply chain. The company's operational excellence is driven by its strict control over the design, manufacturing, and distribution of products.

Vertical Integration: Apple maintains a high degree of vertical integration in its supply chain. By controlling key aspects of its supply chain, such as product design, component sourcing, and assembly, Apple can reduce lead times, maintain high-quality standards, and keep costs in check. The company works closely with suppliers and manufacturers to ensure timely production and delivery of its products.

Global Distribution Network: Apple uses a mix of regional distribution centers, third-party logistics providers, and a robust retail presence to distribute its products globally. Its distribution strategy is built on speed and reliability, ensuring that new products are available in key markets around the world almost simultaneously.

Inventory Management: Apple focuses on keeping its inventory levels low, relying on JIT inventory techniques to reduce the amount of unsold stock and increase product availability. This is especially critical during product launches when demand is high.

Key Takeaways:

Control key elements of your supply chain for better quality control, cost reduction, and speed.

Build a global distribution network that ensures product availability in multiple markets.

Use Just-in-Time (JIT) inventory management to minimize excess stock while maintaining availability.

1.1.4 Maersk: Global Shipping and Supply Chain Leadership

Maersk, one of the largest container shipping companies in the world, has built a logistics strategy focused on global shipping efficiency, technological innovation, and sustainability. As a leader in the shipping industry, Maersk has invested heavily in optimizing operations and expanding its service offerings.

End-to-End Supply Chain Solutions: Maersk offers integrated logistics solutions that span the entire supply chain, from ocean shipping to inland transportation. By providing end-to-end services, Maersk can streamline operations and reduce the complexity that clients face when managing multiple logistics providers.

Technology and Digitalization: Maersk is at the forefront of digitalizing logistics and shipping. The company uses real-time tracking systems to provide visibility into shipments and has implemented blockchain technology for secure, transparent transactions. These innovations help improve the efficiency of the supply chain and reduce the risk of errors or fraud.

Sustainability Efforts: Maersk has committed to becoming carbon-neutral by 2050, focusing on reducing emissions from its fleet and adopting sustainable practices across its operations. The company is investing in new fuel technologies and exploring alternative energy sources to reduce the environmental impact of shipping.

Key Takeaways:

Offer end-to-end supply chain solutions to improve service efficiency and reduce complexity for customers.

Invest in digital technologies to enhance transparency, tracking, and efficiency.

Focus on sustainability and reduce the environmental impact of logistics operations.

1.2 Key Takeaways from Real-World Examples

The case studies of Amazon, Walmart, Apple, and Maersk provide valuable insights into successful logistics strategies. Some of the most important takeaways from these companies include:

1.2.1 Embrace Technology to Improve Efficiency

Across all these companies, technology plays a crucial role in improving logistics efficiency. Whether it's through AI and machine learning, automation, or real-time tracking systems, these companies have successfully leveraged technology to optimize their operations and gain a competitive edge. Investing in digital solutions can help businesses reduce costs, improve speed, and enhance customer satisfaction.

1.2.2 Prioritize Customer-Centric Logistics

All of these companies place a high priority on meeting customer expectations. For example, Amazon's Prime service and Walmart's commitment to reliable inventory management are designed with the customer in mind. By focusing on customer needs, such as fast delivery and product availability, companies can improve satisfaction and build customer loyalty.

1.2.3 Sustainability as a Competitive Advantage

Sustainability is becoming a key factor in logistics excellence. Companies like Maersk are leading the charge with their commitments to reducing carbon emissions and investing in alternative energy sources. Adopting green logistics practices not only helps reduce costs but also enhances a company's brand image in an increasingly environmentally-conscious market.

1.2.4 Foster Strong Supplier Relationships

Strong, collaborative relationships with suppliers are crucial for logistics success. Companies like Walmart and Apple have demonstrated the value of working closely with suppliers to improve inventory accuracy, streamline production, and reduce lead times. Building transparent, mutually beneficial partnerships can significantly enhance supply chain performance.

Case studies of industry leaders like Amazon, Walmart, Apple, and Maersk reveal that logistics excellence is not the result of a single factor, but a combination of technology, customer-focused strategies, supply chain collaboration, and sustainability initiatives. By implementing these best practices and taking strategic actions, companies can enhance their logistics operations, improve cost efficiency, and meet the growing demands of the global marketplace.

Developing a Logistics and Distribution Playbook

A Logistics and Distribution Playbook serves as a comprehensive guide that aligns an organization's logistics strategy with its overall business goals. It integrates critical knowledge from various aspects of logistics and distribution management, providing practical tools, frameworks, and strategies that empower managers to navigate the complexities of logistics operations. In this chapter, we will explore how to develop an effective logistics and distribution playbook, focusing on integrating knowledge, providing actionable tools for managers, and building a robust logistics strategy that ensures success.

1.1 Integrating Knowledge from the Handbook

The first step in developing a logistics and distribution playbook is to integrate key principles and strategies covered in the handbook into a cohesive, actionable plan. The playbook should synthesize the various components of logistics, such as transportation management, warehousing, inventory control, order fulfillment, and risk management, to form a unified strategy.

Mapping Key Areas: Begin by reviewing the major areas discussed in the handbook and identifying the specific challenges and opportunities each area presents for your organization. This includes evaluating the current state of transportation, warehousing, inventory management, and order fulfillment. For example, if the organization struggles with last-mile delivery, it might be necessary to emphasize solutions from that section.

Identifying Organizational Priorities: Focus on the areas that align most closely with the business's immediate and long-term priorities. For instance, if the company's competitive advantage relies on fast delivery, integrating strategies for last-mile delivery and warehouse automation becomes essential.

Customization for Business Needs: Customizing the playbook according to the business's unique needs and industry characteristics is critical. A logistics strategy for a tech company might focus more on technology integration, while a retail-focused company could emphasize supply chain flexibility and customer satisfaction.

Once the key areas are identified, the playbook should incorporate principles from each chapter in the handbook. This means incorporating effective transportation modes, inventory management techniques, warehouse design principles, customer service standards, and risk mitigation strategies.

1.2 Practical Tools and Frameworks for Managers

A playbook is most useful when it provides practical tools and frameworks that managers can directly apply in their day-to-day operations. These tools should help streamline processes, improve decision-making, and enhance overall logistics performance. Below are a few essential tools and frameworks that should be included in the logistics and distribution playbook:

1.2.1 SWOT Analysis for Logistics Strategy

A SWOT (Strengths, Weaknesses, Opportunities, and Threats) analysis is an essential tool for logistics managers to assess the internal and external environment of their logistics operations. By conducting a SWOT analysis, managers can identify key areas for improvement and capitalize on opportunities while mitigating risks.

Strengths: What are the competitive advantages your organization has in its logistics operations? This could be a strong distribution network, efficient warehouse management systems, or strong supplier relationships.

Weaknesses: What challenges are hindering logistics efficiency? Are there bottlenecks in transportation or inventory management? Are there areas of customer service that need improvement?

Opportunities: What external opportunities can be leveraged? Are there emerging technologies, like AI or blockchain, that can optimize logistics? Are there new markets to expand into that require effective logistics solutions?

Threats: What risks should be anticipated? These could include supply chain disruptions, regulatory changes, or environmental challenges such as sustainability requirements.

By regularly conducting a SWOT analysis, logistics managers can adapt their strategies to changing business conditions and better align their logistics operations with broader organizational goals.

1.2.2 Key Performance Indicators (KPIs) and Dashboards

Key Performance Indicators (KPIs) are essential for tracking logistics performance and ensuring that strategies are achieving desired outcomes. A robust logistics playbook will include KPIs specific to transportation, inventory management, warehousing, and customer service.

Transportation KPIs: These may include on-time delivery rate, transportation costs per unit, fuel efficiency, and transportation capacity utilization.

Warehouse KPIs: These may include order accuracy, inventory turnover rate, average warehouse throughput, and storage utilization.

Inventory Management KPIs: These may include inventory turnover, stockout rates, and days of inventory on hand.

Customer Service KPIs: These could include customer satisfaction levels, order fulfillment cycle times, and returns rates.

Dashboards should be included in the playbook to allow managers to monitor these KPIs in real-time. Digital dashboards, integrated with logistics software, provide managers with a bird's-eye view of operations, helping them make data-driven decisions and quickly address any inefficiencies.

1.2.3 Supply Chain Mapping and Flowcharts

Supply chain mapping and flowchart tools help visualize the entire logistics process, from raw material sourcing to final product delivery. These diagrams can be used to identify areas for improvement, bottlenecks, and inefficiencies in the distribution process.

End-to-End Mapping: Create flowcharts that map the entire process from supplier to customer, detailing each step in the supply chain. This includes sourcing, manufacturing, warehousing, distribution, and last-mile delivery.

Process Bottlenecks: Identify areas in the process that are slowing down or adding costs. For example, if the warehousing process is slow due to manual inventory handling, the playbook should emphasize automation solutions.

Decision Trees for Optimization: Build decision trees that guide managers through complex logistics challenges. For instance, when deciding on the mode of transportation for a specific shipment, the decision tree can evaluate factors like cost, speed, and delivery location.

1.2.4 Risk Management Framework

A strong logistics strategy also includes a framework for identifying and mitigating risks. A logistics playbook should have a section dedicated to risk management, helping managers proactively handle potential disruptions.

Risk Assessment Tools: Utilize risk assessment matrices that categorize risks by their likelihood and potential impact on logistics operations. For example, the risk of natural disasters disrupting transportation might be classified as high impact but low likelihood.

Contingency Plans: Develop contingency plans for common risks, such as supply chain disruptions, labor strikes, or customs delays. This may include pre-identified alternate suppliers, rerouting transportation, or stockpiling inventory in advance of seasonal demand spikes.

Business Continuity Plans: A logistics playbook should also integrate business continuity planning, ensuring that in the event of major disruptions, the organization can continue functioning with minimal downtime. This could involve temporary warehousing solutions, alternate transportation providers, or backup communication systems.

1.3 Building a Robust Logistics Strategy

The final element of the playbook is the development of a robust logistics strategy that ties together all the concepts, tools, and frameworks. A well-defined strategy ensures that logistics operations are not only efficient but also aligned with the overall goals of the organization.

1.3.1 Aligning Logistics with Corporate Strategy

A logistics strategy should be aligned with the broader business objectives of the company. For example, if the company's goal is to expand into new markets, the logistics strategy should prioritize building flexible distribution networks, ensuring scalability in transportation, and investing in international shipping capabilities. Aligning logistics with corporate goals helps ensure that the logistics function supports rather than hinders growth.

1.3.2 Setting Clear Objectives and Milestones

The logistics strategy should include specific, measurable objectives and key milestones. These may include reducing transportation costs by 10% over the next year, improving warehouse throughput by 15%, or achieving 95% on-time delivery rates. Setting these clear objectives helps ensure that logistics managers can focus their efforts and track progress toward goals.

1.3.3 Continuous Improvement Culture

Building a robust logistics strategy involves embracing a culture of continuous improvement. The playbook should encourage managers to constantly evaluate operations, identify inefficiencies, and implement improvements. This could be through tools like Six Sigma, Kaizen, or Total Quality Management (TQM), which provide frameworks for ongoing optimization.

1.3.4 Leveraging Technology for Scalability

Technology plays a critical role in scaling logistics operations. The playbook should include guidance on selecting and integrating logistics software systems, such as Transportation Management Systems (TMS), Warehouse Management Systems (WMS), and Enterprise Resource Planning (ERP) tools. These systems not only streamline operations but also provide the necessary data to make informed decisions.

Developing a Logistics and Distribution Playbook is essential for providing managers with a comprehensive, actionable guide to optimize logistics operations. By integrating knowledge from various aspects of logistics, providing practical tools like KPIs, flowcharts, and risk management frameworks, and building a robust strategy aligned with corporate goals, the playbook serves as a roadmap for achieving logistics excellence. It ensures that logistics operations are efficient, scalable, and capable of supporting business growth and customer satisfaction in a rapidly changing market.

"Success in logistics and distribution is built on precision, planning, and perseverance. Every challenge is an opportunity to optimize, innovate, and drive progress. With the right strategies, the journey from complexity to efficiency becomes the path to limitless growth."

www.ingramcontent.com/pod-product-compliance
Lightning Source LLC
Chambersburg PA
CBHW071022240526
45469CB00006BD/2044